Thinking Strategies

for the

Successful Classroom

9–11 Year Olds

Contributors:

Rosalind Curtis

Maiya Edwards

Fay Holbert

Margaret Bishop

Brilliant Publications

Publisher's Information

Brilliant Publications
www.brilliantpublications.co.uk

Sales
BEBC (Brilliant Publications)
Albion Close, Parkstone, Poole, Dorset, BH12 3LL, UK
Tel: 01202 712910   Fax: 0845 1309300

Editorial
Unit 10, Sparrow Hall Farm,
Edlesborough
Dunstable, Bedfordshire, LU6 2ES, UK
Tel: 01525 222292   Fax: 01525 222720

Illustrations by Greg Anderson-Clift
Cover design by Lynda Murray
Cover illustration by Sharon Scotland

Acknowledgements: Blake Education and Brilliant Publications would like to thank Professor Joseph Renzulli and Professor Howard Gardner for permission to base some of the activities in this book on their theories. Professor Gardner's theories can be found in: Gardner, H, *Intelligence Reframed* (New York, Basic Books, 1999).

Contents

Introduction

The teaching and management strategies in this book cater for all pupils, but provide in-built opportunities for bright pupils. Just like pupils who are struggling, bright pupils have needs that must be met before they can develop personally and academically to their full potential. Some of the consequences of not catering adequately for these pupils are frustration, disruptive or aggressive behaviour, withdrawal and underachievement.

These strategies allow all pupils to actively participate in their own learning. Worksheets and task cards are ready to use or can easily be added to your existing teaching programme.

How This Book is Structured

Management Strategies for Developing Higher-level Thinking in the Mainstream Classroom

This section describes the key management strategies for developing higher-level thinking in your classroom. Each management strategy is given a symbol which appears on the task cards and photocopiable worksheets throughout the book. In this section you'll also find helpful generic photocopiable worksheets to support these management strategies.

Teaching Strategies

Six teaching strategies are targeted:
◆ Bloom's Taxonomy
◆ Creative Thinking
◆ Research Skills
◆ Questioning Skills and Brainstorming
◆ Renzulli's Enrichment Triad
◆ Gardner's Multiple Intelligences

Each of these strategies has its own section including:

Notes These provide an overview of the methodology of the teaching strategy and its practical application in the classroom.

Activities These include a wide range of teaching activities covering the main Learning Areas. They can be undertaken exclusively, or in conjunction with activities from the other teaching-strategy sections. They could also prompt you to develop your own activities.

Task Cards and Worksheets The activities are supported by a variety of ready-to-use worksheets and task cards. Suggested management strategies are indicated by symbols in the top right-hand corner.

Management Strategies for Developing Higher-level Thinking in the Mainstream Classroom

by **Maiya Edwards**

Management Strategies for Developing Higher-level Thinking in the Mainstream Classroom

As a teacher, it is difficult to predict the skills that will be of value to pupils in the future. Teaching them higher-level thinking strategies will provide them with the tools necessary to navigate through the inevitable information overload and help them determine what information is of use to them.

Linda Silverman, the director of the Gifted Development Center in Denver, suggests that there are several approaches which work well when dealing with bright pupils in the classroom. These approaches, listed below, work equally well with all pupils and will help to create a classroom environment that fosters higher-order thinking skills.

Find out what they know before you teach them

This will prevent reteaching what a pupil already knows.

Remove drill from their lives

Bright pupils learn and retain a concept the first time it is presented to them. Allow them to move on to something else while you consolidate concepts with the rest of the class.

Pace instruction at the rate of the learner

Pupils learn at different rates. Allow them to progress at their own rate.

Use discovery learning techniques

Use Inductive Learning strategies (such as those explained in the Bloom's Taxonomy model) to allow pupils to use thinking skills to reach conclusions.

Allow them to arrive at answers in their own way

Bright pupils enjoy devising their own problem-solving techniques.

Allow pupils to form their own co-operative learning groups

Avoid always making the brightest pupil in the group responsible for the whole group's learning. Allow them to sometimes choose their own groups and work with other bright, motivated pupils.

Design an individual education plan

This will cater for different learning rates.

Teach them the art of argument

Since bright pupils have a tendency to argue anyway, teach them to understand when it is appropriate to argue and also to understand the reaction of others to their argumentativeness.

Allow pupils to observe

Provide pupils with opportunities to observe and don't demand immediate answers.

Be flexible in designing programmes

Provide your pupils with a variety of programme alternatives, such as independent study, special classes, mentoring and enrichment and extension activities.

As many bright pupils are unable to achieve their full potential in the regular classroom, they can often become frustrated and begin to exhibit disruptive or aggressive behaviour. Others withdraw from class activities, or deliberately mask their ability.

Providing activities for the entire class does not mean that the activities need to limit bright pupils to make them conform. These classroom-management strategies have been devised to allow for implementation of all of the key educational qualities referred to above. The strategies are practical, flexible and easy to implement.

Each strategy has been given an easily recognizable symbol (see the next four pages) so that when these strategies are applied to the task card and worksheet activities in this book, you will know immediately how to organize your classroom.

Management Strategies for Developing Higher-level Thinking in the Mainstream Classroom

A range of classroom-management strategies could be employed to promote and encourage the development of the talent of the pupils in your class. Any of the strategies listed below would help to achieve a positive classroom environment.

Management Strategies Suitable for the Mainstream Classroom

 Enrichment and Extension Activities

 Learning/Interest Centres

 Contracts

 Independent Research

 Parent Involvement

 Peer Tutoring

Competitions and Awards

Mentoring

Team Teaching

Withdrawal from Classroom

 Mixed-ability Grouping

 Same-ability Grouping

 Vertical Grouping

 Field Trips

Below is a sample page from the sections that follow. The symbols relating to the classroom strategies are at the top of each worksheet or task card.

These symbols indicate the best strategies to use.

The learning area utilized for the activity.

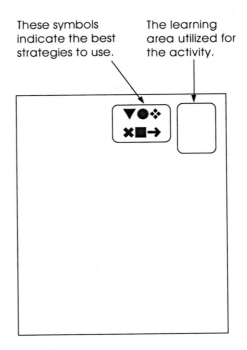

Other broader strategies less suitable for the classroom are listed below.

Management Strategies Suitable for the Whole-School Approach

♦ Liaison with feeder secondary school

♦ Out-of-school same-ability groups

♦ In-school same-ability groups

♦ Camps

♦ Specialist classes

♦ Extra-curricular activities

♦ Competitions and awards

Class Programming

♦ Curriculum compacting

♦ Acceleration

Management Strategies for Developing Higher-level Thinking in the Mainstream Classroom

1 ▼ Enrichment and Extension Activities

These can be provided in all subject areas in a variety of ways:

- ◆ Task cards or worksheets for higher-level thinking skills
- ◆ Research tasks
- ◆ Special 'challenge' days
- ◆ Independent projects
- ◆ Parent or mentor involvement

2 → Learning/Interest Centres

These can be established in a corner of the classroom, and designed to generate interest in a particular topic. They can:

- ◆ Concentrate on one specific aspect of work being studied, such as 'Weather Patterns'
- ◆ Accommodate a special interest, such as 'Dinosaurs'
- ◆ Extend certain skills, such as Advanced Language/Mathematical Skills or Thinking Skills

See worksheets 4, 5, 6

3 ● Contracts

Pupils can be given a range of activities to complete which are set out around the room. Each pupil is given a list of the activities and asked to mark off each one as it is completed. The flexibility of this contract system appeals to the more capable pupil.

Contracts also have the advantage of being either teacher initiated or pupil initiated. The teacher can set defined, targeted tasks or can allow the pupils to pursue their own interests with some guidance. There is also flexibility

in the time allowed for the contracts. A contract can be extended over many weeks or set as a one night task.

See worksheets 1, 2, 3, 4, 7

4 ❖ Independent Research

Independent research provides an opportunity either within the school day or over a longer period to develop personal competencies through individual experiences. It may also involve interaction with others when appropriate. The research topic can be teacher initiated or pupil initiated.

It allows the pupil to launch an in-depth investigation into something that they want to find out more about without constant supervision. It also encourages the pupil to use self-initiative and to employ their own style of learning to produce results.

The teacher's role changes from being the source of all knowledge to that of a facilitator and consultant.

See worksheets 1, 2, 3, 4, 7

5 ■ Parent Involvement

Establishing and maintaining a register of parents' interests, abilities and availability can be invaluable when planning a work- activities scheme for the brighter pupils in the classroom. Parents can be used to supervise same-ability groups or extension activities and to encourage the exploration of individual interest areas. Some of the ways that parents could be kept abreast of classroom activities are newsletters, resource packs and information evenings.

See worksheet 9

6 ✖ Peer Tutoring

The more capable pupils can be paired with underachievers for some activities. This can be mutually beneficial for both pupils. The brighter pupils must develop an ability to clearly communicate an understanding of a topic or problem, while the underachiever receives the benefit of one-to-one coaching.

Outside the mainstream classroom, you can pair more able, older pupils with bright, younger pupils. For example, pairing Year 6 pupils with Year 1 pupils works particularly well. The pupils could be paired for 30 to 60 minutes per week for activities such as writing, ICT, art or thinking games.

7 ★ Competitions and Awards

Competition and Award schemes such as 'Young Innovator of the Year' and 'Tournament of the Minds' offer enrichment opportunities for all pupils, but particularly the brighter pupils. Pupils within the mainstream classroom could be provided with activities to prepare them for these tournaments and competitions.

Intra-class competitions and awards are a dynamic means of extending the entire class. There is a wide range of options, of which some are:

◆ 30-minute quiz challenges.
◆ Knock-out quiz challenges throughout the term or year.
◆ Award schemes for independent research tasks. (Bronze award for a written and pictorial presentation; Silver if something extra is included, such as a model, video or web page; and Gold if the project is outstanding.)
◆ Individual point scoring for tasks throughout the year. This scheme works well for all pupils in the mainstream classroom, as points can be awarded for outstanding work, additional work, improvement, effort, positive attitudes or helping others. Points can be exchanged for play money at the end of each term,

and pupils can bid at a class auction for donated items (such as books, tickets or toys) or 'buy' privileges, such as extra computer time.

8 ◗ Mentoring

These schemes link individual pupils with community members who have expertise in certain areas. Teachers can establish their own database of suitable people or seek the assistance of their Regional Partnership of the National Academy for Gifted and Talented Youth. Mentors can also talk to the class on given interest areas and participate in some follow-up activities. This is a very productive way of inspiring excellence and encouraging independent interests.

9 ✳ Team Teaching

Pupils with various interests and talents meet with different teachers who specialize in specific subject areas. An excellent way to implement this is for three teachers to nominate three different fields of interest. The pupils then select which area of interest to pursue. This can be timetabled into the standard teaching week and run for two or three lessons, with suitable assessment regime its conclusion.

10 ✦ Withdrawal from Classroom

Very exceptional pupils (or 'gifted' pupils) can be withdrawn from a mixed-ability class for instruction with other more advanced pupils. This instruction can be provided by a specially appointed teacher or tutor, or a volunteer.

Management Strategies for Developing Higher-level Thinking in the Mainstream Classroom

11 ⊃ Mixed-ability Grouping

When working on class assignments, the pupils are placed in groups with a range of abilities. The more able pupils assume the leadership roles, with the others given the tasks of writing and reporting. Roles can also be interchangeable, or they can be rotated so that an even amount of work is done in all aspects of a task. An ideal number for mixed-ability groupings is three to five.

See worksheet 4

12 ✚ Same-ability Grouping

All pupils can be grouped according to their relative ability in the classroom. Higher-ability pupils can occasionally be grouped for full-time instruction within a mixed-ability classroom. This works well when compacting a curriculum for the brighter pupils so that they are able to progress at their own rate.

13 ▲ Vertical Grouping

In classrooms that already contain several year groups, bright pupils of different ages can be combined with others who have similar interests, abilities and aptitudes.

See worksheet 4

14 ♣ Field Trips

This involves off-campus excursions to meet with experts in various fields, for example museum experts, marine biologists or geologists. Field trips can provide an excellent basis for both same-ability group projects or independent research projects.

Self-evaluation

It should be remembered that self-evaluation is a very powerful form of assessment and should be an essential component of every classroom evaluation process.

This has been incorporated into the worksheets on the following pages.

Worksheets

A range of worksheets has been provided which can be used to assess and encourage pupils when using the above management strategies.

They are not activities in themselves but are designed to support the various teaching strategies presented in the book.

Teacher Records

For your own records and so that you can show parents that you have given their child the opportunity to express the full range of skills, we have provided an individual record sheet suitable for each pupil as well as a class record sheet.

See worksheets 7 and 8

Name: _____

My Research Contract

Research Title: _____

Starting Date: _____   Completion Date: _____

Subject Area: _____

Brief Description: _____

Resources to be used: _____

Method of final presentation: _____

School time allocated to independent research: _____

Home time allocated to independent research: _____

Pupil's Signature: _____

Teacher's Signature: _____

Self-evaluation

The best thing about my independent research was: _____

_____

_____

The thing I found hardest to do was: _____

_____

_____

I could improve this by: _____

_____

_____

Teacher Comment

Name:

My Contract

My contract is to _____

I will start on _____ and finish by _____

✓ When finished	What I will do	How I feel about my work

Teacher Comment

My Research Checklist

Tick (✓) the methods you have used for your independent research and hand this sheet in with your final presentation.

☐ Brainstorming

☐ Concept Mapping

☐ Library Research

☐ Interviewing

☐ Survey

☐ Questionnaire

☐ Experiment

☐ Graphs/Tables

Your final methods of presentation can be very simple or quite complex. Here are some suggestions. Circle the methods you will use.

- Written Report
- Videotape
- Collection
- Letter
- Musical Composition

- Model
- Demonstration
- Scrapbook
- Play/TV Show
- Advertisement

- Comic Strip
- Magazine
- Computer Program
- Panel Discussion
- Invention

☐ Final Presentation

☐ Own Evaluation of the Independent Study

☐ Teacher Evaluation of the Independent Study

Self-evaluation

Name:

Checklist for Group Work

Other Group Members: _____

☐ I contributed new ideas. The best idea was _____

☐ I listened to the ideas of others. The best idea was _____

☐ I encouraged others in my group. This was by _____

☐ Something I could improve on is _____

_____

_____

Name:

Questionnaire for Learning/Interest Centres or Enrichment Activities

Task: _____ Time taken: _____

How I did the activity and what I thought of it: _____

_____

_____

Future activities I would like included: _____

_____

_____

Name:

Learning/Interest Centre Evaluation Sheet

ACTIVITY	DATE COMPLETED	EVALUATION (for example: too hard, too easy, boring, interesting)

Teacher Comment

Name:

Concept Mapping

IDEA

IDEA

IDEA

IDEA

SUB-TOPIC

_____

SUB-TOPIC

_____

TOPIC

_____

SUB-TOPIC

_____

SUB-TOPIC

_____

IDEA

IDEA

IDEA

IDEA

Thinking Strategies for the Successful Classroom, 9–11 Year Olds

Brilliant Publications

Individual Record Sheet

Extension Procedures

Pupil Name: _____   Year: _____

Pupils should complete one task card or worksheet from each extension activity.

THINKING STRATEGY	TASK CARDS/WORKSHEETS COMPLETED (Indicate worksheet numbers as appropriate)
Bloom's Taxonomy (BT)	
Creative Thinking (CT)	
Research Skills (R)	
Questioning/Brainstorming (QB)	
Renzulli's Enrichment Triad (RT)	
Gardner's Multiple Intelligences (GI)	

Teacher Comment

Class Record Sheet
Extension Procedures

Check that each pupil has completed at least one task card or worksheet from each extension procedure.

PUPIL'S NAME	BT	CT	R	QB	RT	GI	COMMENT

Brilliant Publications

© Blake Education Pty Ltd. 2004

Register of Parents' Interests

PARENT'S NAME	CHILD	CONTACT DETAILS	AVAILABILITY	AREA/S OF INTEREST

Bloom's Taxonomy

by **Maiya Edwards**

Overview for the Classroom Teacher

Bloom's Taxonomy

This model is one of the most frequently used extension procedures for the development of higher-level thinking skills. These skills are applicable to any subject, and to any level of education from pre-school to higher education. Many varied teaching and learning activities can be developed using this as the basis.

The model enables *all* pupils to work through the process of developing a concept, with the more advanced pupils spending longer at the higher levels than the average pupil.

The thought processes involved in the different levels are:

1.   KNOWLEDGE – recognize, list, name, read, absorb.

2.   COMPREHENSION – restate, describe, identify, review, explain.

3.   APPLICATION – apply, illustrate, connect, develop, use.

4.   ANALYSIS – interpret, categorize, contrast, compare, classify.

5.   SYNTHESIS – plan, create, invent, modify, revise.

6.   EVALUATION – judge, recommend, assess, criticize, justify.

Average Pupil

1.   Knowing and recalling specific facts.

2.   Understanding the meaning from given information.

3.   Using previously learned information in new situations.

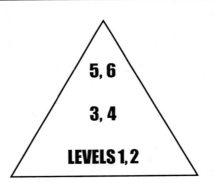

Talented Pupil

4.   Breaking up the whole into parts.

5.   Putting together the parts to form a new whole.

6.   Making value judgements.

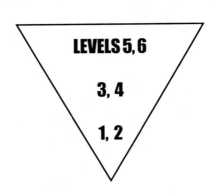

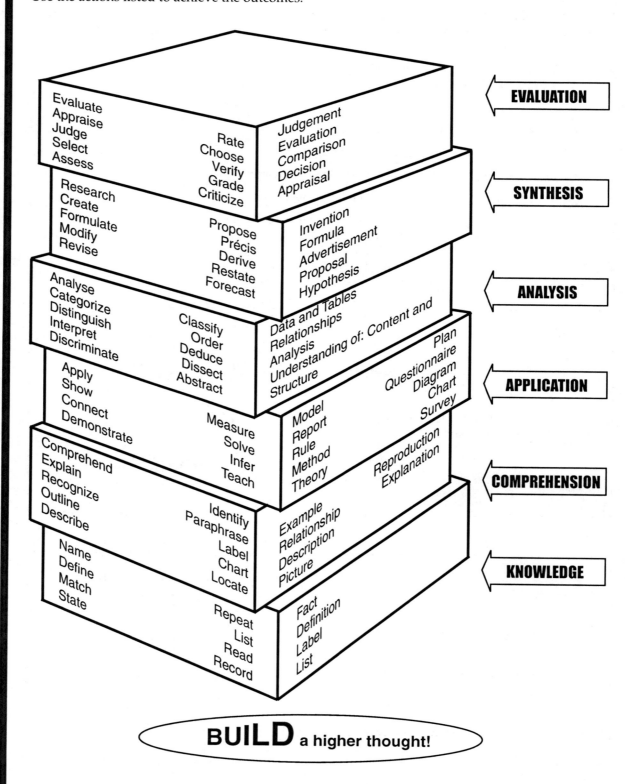

Overview for the Classroom Teacher

From Convergent to Divergent Thinking

Use the actions listed to achieve the outcomes.

EVALUATION

Evaluate
Appraise
Judge
Select
Assess

Rate
Choose
Verify
Grade
Criticize

Judgement
Evaluation
Comparison
Decision
Appraisal

SYNTHESIS

Research
Create
Formulate
Modify
Revise

Propose
Précis
Derive
Restate
Forecast

Invention
Formula
Advertisement
Proposal
Hypothesis

ANALYSIS

Analyse
Categorize
Distinguish
Interpret
Discriminate

Classify
Order
Deduce
Dissect
Abstract

Data and Tables
Relationships
Analysis
Understanding of: Content and
Structure

APPLICATION

Apply
Show
Connect
Demonstrate

Measure
Solve
Infer
Teach

Model
Report
Rule
Method
Theory

Plan
Questionnaire
Diagram
Chart
Survey

COMPREHENSION

Comprehend
Explain
Recognize
Outline
Describe

Identify
Paraphrase
Label
Chart
Locate

Example
Relationship
Description
Picture

Reproduction
Explanation

KNOWLEDGE

Name
Define
Match
State

Repeat
List
Read
Record

Fact
Definition
Label
List

BUILD a higher thought!

Bloom's Taxonomy in Literacy

Theme: Humour in Writing

Knowledge

◆ Ask pupils to brainstorm the sort of things that make them laugh.

◆ Ask pupils to name some of the humorous books they have read.

Comprehension

◆ Pupils can retell some of the funny stories they have read.

◆ Ask them to describe some of the humorous characters in the books.

Application

◆ Cut out some cartoon characters and paste them on a sheet of paper. Ask pupils to work in groups to list the characteristics of each character. For example: Lucy from 'Peanuts' could be described as bossy, loud and opinionated. Give each group three characters and encourage them to write a comprehensive list of characteristics.

◆ Ask pupils to write a report on a humorous book they have read.

◆ Study the style of limericks and humorous poems in general. Have pupils write their own versions. (See Task Cards pages 26–27 for ideas.)

Analysis

◆ Ask pupils to identify what makes a book or character funny.

◆ Ask them to think of some of the humorous things the characters did or said.

◆ Write a biography of an author of humorous books.

Synthesis

◆ Brainstorm a list of original or bizarre things to sell. Examples could be: birthday parties on the moon, ice-cream pizzas or back-to-front shoes. Challenge pupils to write an advertisement for their product.

◆ Ask pupils to make up their own funny character to do the sales pitch for their advertisement. Ask them to role-play the character to the rest of the class.

◆ Pupils can make up a funny advertising jingle about something that they like to eat.

◆ Cut out a variety of different cartoon characters and challenge pupils to create a new cartoon of their own.

Evaluation

◆ Ask pupils to write a book review about their favourite humorous book.

◆ Ask pupils if there are some things they believe shouldn't be made fun of. Why?

◆ Form a panel to choose the 10 funniest poems or jokes from those submitted by the class.

BLOOM'S
TAXONOMY
Literacy
Worksheet 10

Name:

Management
Strategies:
▼ →
● ❖

Future of the UK

Comprehension

Write a brief outline of some of the changes that have taken place in your lifetime.

_____

_____

_____

_____

_____

_____

_____

_____

_____

_____

_____

_____

_____

_____

_____

_____

_____

Knowledge

Make a timeline of important events in British history.

Year   Event

_____   _____

_____   _____

_____   _____

_____   _____

_____   _____

_____   _____

_____   _____

_____   _____

Application

Illustrate one

of the changes

in a cartoon strip.

The Future of Britain

Future of the UK

Analysis

Design a questionnaire that will help to discover what British people expect of the future.

_____

_____

_____

_____

_____

_____

_____

Evaluation

Select 3 major problems facing the UK today.

1. _____

2. _____

3. _____

What are your solutions?

_____

_____

_____

_____

_____

_____

_____

_____

_____

_____

_____

_____

Synthesis

Design a school of the future that would really appeal to children. Sketch and label some of your ideas below.

Bloom's Taxonomy in Literacy

Analysis, Synthesis, Evaluation

BLOOM'S TAXONOMY
Literacy
TASK CARDS

Magic and Make-believe

What if Cinderella's Fairy Godmother could perform some magic for the Three Little Pigs and the Big Bad Wolf? What do you think they would ask for?

Computer Complaints

If computers could talk, what do you think would be the 10 major complaints they would have?

Alice in the Future

Retitle the story Alice in Wonderland and set it in the year 2050.

My Invention

What funny invention could this be?

Bloom's Taxonomy in Literacy

Application, Analysis, Synthesis, Evaluation

Come to My Party!

Make up a party list of your five
favourite humorous characters.
Design some party games
they may like to play.

A Modern Nursery Rhyme

Here is one version of a
traditional nursery rhyme
placed in a modern-day setting:
Little Jack Horner
Sat in a corner
Working on his PC
As he checked his e-mail
He let out a wail
'No one is writing to me!'
Choose your own nursery rhyme
and adapt it to the present day.

What a Stink!

The answer is 'Stinky Socks'!

Write five questions.

A Funny Speech

Your favourite funny character
has been asked to give
a talk at your school.
Write out his/her speech.

Bloom's Taxonomy in Maths

Knowledge

◆ Explain and demonstrate mathematical concepts using practical and real-life situations (for example, pupils using one colour then adding two others, or two pupils sharing six pencils).

◆ Encourage discussion between pupils and between pupils and the teacher. Pupils who grasp concepts more quickly should be encouraged to help the slower pupils.

◆ Ensure pupils have regular practice in fundamental number skills. A certain time would be set aside each day for this.

◆ Have pupils develop automatic recall of number facts. Use a combination of tables, games and everyday problems. For example 2 x 2 = 4 of the two-times- table could be reinforced using an everyday problem such as: 'Tim and Sara each have two blocks. How many are there altogether?'

Comprehension

◆ Working in pairs, ask pupils to take turns in demonstrating number facts to each other using concrete representation. For example, 163 x 2 could be demonstrated using MAB blocks.

Application

◆ Encourage pupils to transfer their skills to other subject areas. For example, they could apply measuring, estimating and the use of shapes when making models or charts. This would transfer their mathematical skills to other subjects such as Science, Humanities or Art.

◆ Allow pupils to work in groups to list all the situations in their home where they would use calculations. Examples would be: count money, estimate time and add up bills.

◆ Ask all of the pupils to think of a question for which the answer could be written as a graph. For example 'How many days has it rained this week?'

Analysis

◆ Stimulate pupils to think about their number problems with questions like: 'What would happen to this number if you left out a zero?' 'Where might this measurement be used in real life?' 'How did you arrive at that answer?'

◆ Ask pupils to use the telephone directory to find phone numbers which add up to 30.

◆ Pupils can work in pairs to explain fractions to their partner using pieces of paper. They could start with simple fractions such as one half or one quarter and proceed to more complex fractions.

Synthesis

◆ Ask pupils to think of 10 uses for a metre of string.

◆ Ask pupils to work in groups to design a Quiz Show based on numbers.

◆ Draw a picture using only straight lines.

Evaluation

◆ Brainstorm all the reasons why estimating is an essential skill to have.

◆ Pupils can recommend some changes to the present maths curriculum based on things they have studied earlier in the year.

Bloom's Taxonomy in Maths

Analysis, Synthesis, Evaluation

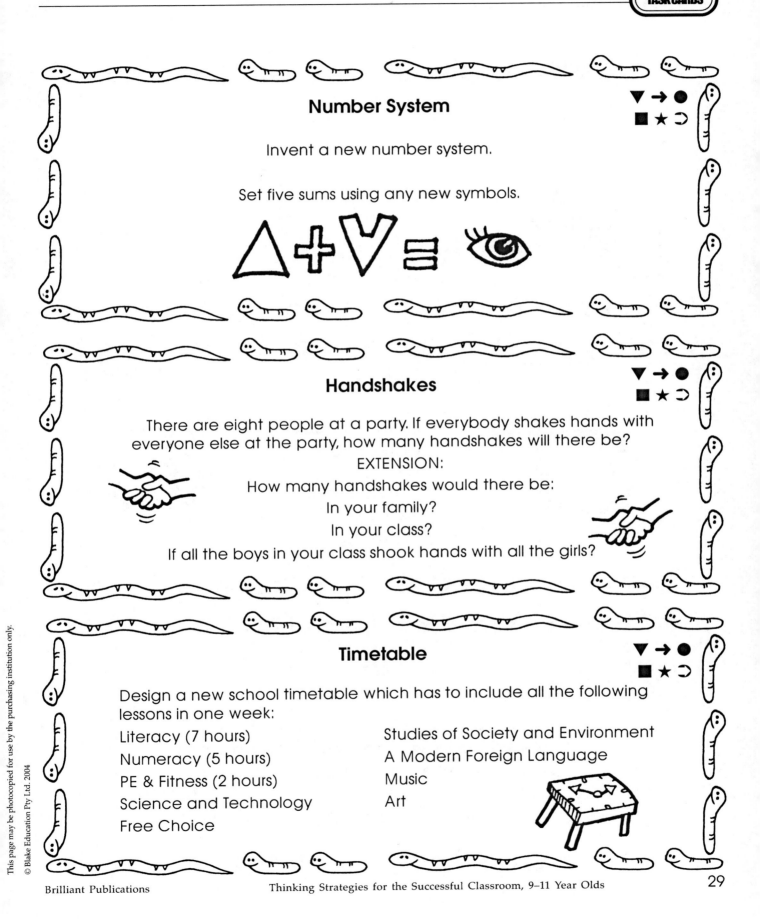

Number System

Invent a new number system.

Set five sums using any new symbols.

Handshakes

There are eight people at a party. If everybody shakes hands with everyone else at the party, how many handshakes will there be?

EXTENSION:

How many handshakes would there be:

In your family?

In your class?

If all the boys in your class shook hands with all the girls?

Timetable

Design a new school timetable which has to include all the following lessons in one week:

Literacy (7 hours)

Numeracy (5 hours)

PE & Fitness (2 hours)

Science and Technology

Free Choice

Studies of Society and Environment

A Modern Foreign Language

Music

Art

Bloom's Taxonomy in Maths

Analysis and Synthesis

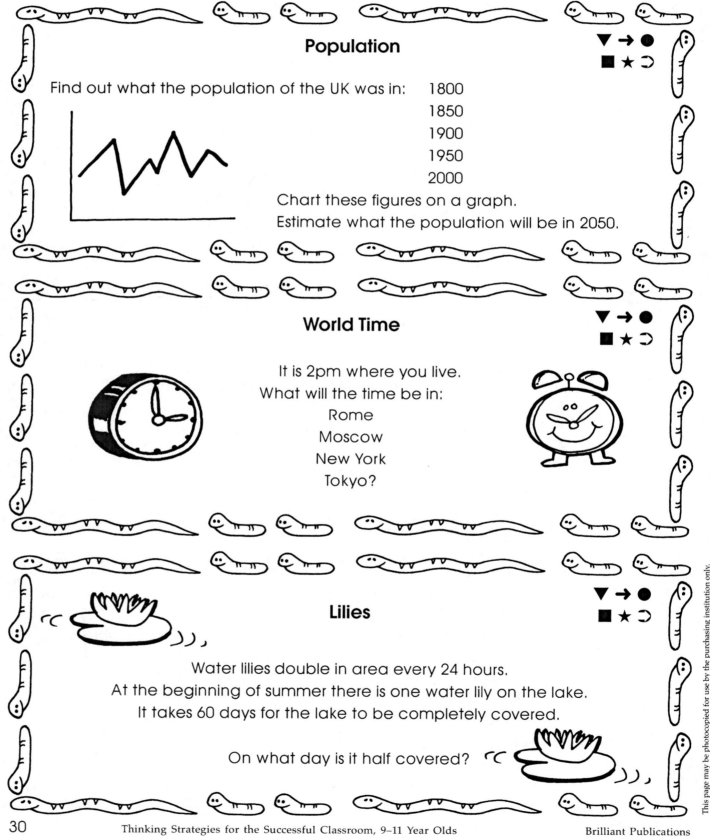

Population

Find out what the population of the UK was in:

1800
1850
1900
1950
2000

Chart these figures on a graph.
Estimate what the population will be in 2050.

World Time

It is 2pm where you live.
What will the time be in:
Rome
Moscow
New York
Tokyo?

Lilies

Water lilies double in area every 24 hours.
At the beginning of summer there is one water lily on the lake.
It takes 60 days for the lake to be completely covered.

On what day is it half covered?

Name:

Maths Research Tasks

Management
Strategies:
❖ ✖

Application,
Analysis, Synthesis

BLOOM'S
TAXONOMY
Maths
Worksheet 12

Here are some problems for you to research.
They all require a prediction and then the right answer.

1   How much money is there in three metres of 10 pence pieces laid out in a line?

My prediction is _____

The answer is _____

2   How many words are on the front page of today's newspaper?

My prediction is _____

The answer is _____

3   How many bricks are on the outside structure of the school building?

My prediction is _____

How I calculated the right answer _____

_____

The answer is _____

4   How high is the tallest part of the school?

My prediction is _____

How I calculated the right answer _____

_____

The answer is _____

5   How much space is needed to store a collection of 300 CDs?

My prediction is _____

How I calculated the right answer _____

_____

The answer is _____

Name:

Management Strategies:

▼ ★

Number Trivia

How many number questions can you answer?

1 Who is code-named **007**? _____

2 How many 'dog years' are there for every human year?

3 How many years in: One decade?   _____

One score?   _____

One century?   _____

One millennium?   _____

4 How many cards in a full deck, excluding Jokers? _____

5 What is a **747**? _____

6 Who wrote:

20 000 Leagues Under the Sea?   _____

Around the World in **80** Days?   _____

101 Dalmatians?   _____

1984?   _____

7 Think of 3 questions of your own.

Bloom's Taxonomy in Science

Theme: Pollution

Knowledge

◆ Challenge the class to define what pollution is.

◆ List the different types of pollution such as air, noise and water.

◆ Read about the causes and effects of pollution. Ask the pupils to list them under 'Cause' (for example car exhaust fumes) and 'Effect' (for example smog, asthma).

◆ Brainstorm things that are being done to combat the effects of pollution: in the UK, in your county, in your town or local area.

Comprehension

◆ Ask pupils to provide a definition of pollution.

◆ Ask pupils to select one type of pollution and describe it in detail.

◆ Pupils can create a collage of the effects of pollution.

Application

◆ Encourage pupils to give examples of pollution from their own experience. Ask them questions like: 'What examples of pollution are you aware of in your local community?' 'Why is it a problem?' 'How long has it been a problem?' 'What attempts have been made to clean up the pollution?' 'How successful have the efforts to solve the problems been?'

◆ Ask pupils to choose one type of pollution in their local area and depict its effects by means of photographs, an illustration or a model.

Analysis

◆ Encourage pupils to analyse the main problems caused by the pollution they have discussed. Ask them to present a list of possible solutions to attach to their model or illustration.

◆ Ask pupils to examine their household waste and then construct a graph to show the different categories.

Synthesis

◆ Ask pupils to predict how the UK could change as a result of increased air and water pollution.

◆ Allow pupils to work in groups of four or five to produce a short play about one major problem caused by pollution.

Evaluation

◆ Ask pupils to choose one example of pollution in their local area that they consider to be a serious problem. Ask them to write a letter outlining their concerns and providing possible solutions.

Name:

Management
Strategies:

City of the Future

Application, Synthesis

TASK 1: DESIGN a model of a **City of the Future** which will have no pollution problems.

TASK 2: EXPLAIN how you would solve potential pollution problems in your city.

My **City of the Future** would be called _____

POTENTIAL PROBLEM	SOLUTION
Household waste	
Polluted drinking water	
Air pollution from cars	
Air pollution from factories	
Noise pollution from cars and planes	

Teacher Comment

Name:

Pollution

1 Pollution is a necessary part of modern life. Agree / Disagree

JUSTIFICATION:

_____

_____

2 Household waste can easily be reduced. Agree / Disagree

JUSTIFICATION:

_____

_____

3 Pollution is not a problem in our local environment. Agree / Disagree

JUSTIFICATION:

_____

_____

4 The media exaggerates pollution problems. Agree / Disagree

JUSTIFICATION:

_____

_____

5 All countries should use nuclear power
because it produces cheap electricity. Agree / Disagree

JUSTIFICATION:

_____

_____

Teacher Comment

Bloom's Taxonomy in Creative Arts

Theme: Folk Music

Knowledge

◆ Talk about traditional folk music in the UK and invite a discussion about how folk music varies around the world with different types ranging from traditional to contemporary styles. Ask pupils how much folk music they have heard. Discuss the results.

◆ Can pupils list the musical instruments of folk origin from around the world. Ask them to describe the types of sounds they make.

Comprehension

◆ Ask pupils to give examples of contemporary folk music.

◆ Play some contemporary and some traditional folk music to the class. Ask pupils to locate which instruments are being used in different pieces of music.

Application

◆ Find or make an instrument which can create a sound you might hear in traditional folk music. Write these sounds down and play them.

◆ Survey the class to find out their favourite folk music.

Analysis

◆ Search the school library for compact disks or audio tapes of folk music groups. You can also visit music internet sites such as **www.goodnoise.com**. Compare traditional folk music to *Rock and Roll*, *Country and Western*, *Soul* and *Hip-hop*. Ask pupils to record similarities and differences as you play the music.

◆ Play a traditional piece of folk music, such as Aboriginal music, and ask pupils to discuss its origin. Ask the pupils to try to interpret its meaning.

◆ Read the class a selection of Dreaming stories recommended by your school librarian. Analyse the features of a Dreaming story. Have pupils record various sounds of nature (such as rain, wind or rustling leaves) and ask them to decide which would be suitable as the background music for a Dreaming story.

Synthesis

◆ Ask pupils to investigate how they can use things around them to produce music. For example bird calls, blowing across glass bottles.

◆ Read the story of *The Rainbow Serpent* to the class. Discuss how it is an ancient Dreaming story which tells how outback mountain ranges and rivers were formed. Talk about what sort of music would suit each character. Create rhythms to represent the changing moods of different parts of the story. For example, the happy times at the beginning of the story and the destruction caused by the angry Rainbow Serpent later in the story.

◆ Ask pupils to plan a Folk Music Day. Contact a local folk band to advise you on indigenous music and culture. Ask them to come in and talk to pupils and assist in the planning. Aim for a balance of contemporary and traditional music.

Evaluation

◆ Pupils can judge folk singers or bands from their most to least favourite. Ask them to justify their ranking.

◆ Evaluate the success of your Folk Music Day and decide what you could do to improve it.

Name:

Rainbow Serpent

TASK 1: Use folk symbols to create a colourful Rainbow Serpent.

TASK 2: Write a song about the Rainbow Serpent from the point of view of the folk community in the story.

TASK 3:
Write a song about the Rainbow Serpent from the serpent's point of view.

TASK 4: List the musical instruments you will use to accompany your song.

Teacher Comment

Bloom's Taxonomy in Creative Arts

Application, Analysis, Synthesis, Evaluation

Musical Instrument

What sort of
musical instruments
could you make using some
of the following?
paper, card, comb,
elastic bands, rice, plastic
bottles

Planning an Escape

If you were stranded
on a desert island
with only a recorder,
clapping sticks and
cymbals,
how would you use these
to help you escape?

Yothu Yindi

The answer is Yothu Yindi.

Make up six questions.

Alphabet Music

For each letter of the
alphabet try to name a
musical instrument.

Make Your Own Task Cards

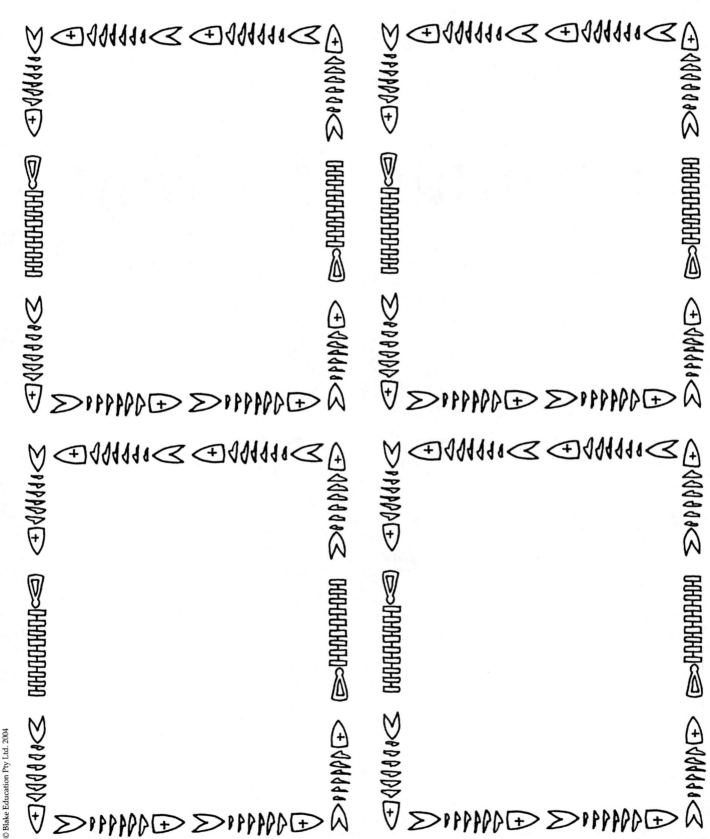

Creative Thinking

by **Maiya Edwards**

Overview for the Classroom Teacher

Creative Thinking Skills

In this section, we are trying to move away from verbal and deductive skills and convergent thinking at factual levels to encourage originality, inductive and inferential skills and divergent thinking.

By recognizing and encouraging the potential of creative thinking in the classroom, the teacher can equip pupils with the open-ended, divergent thinking skills that are so useful in an ever-changing world.

Creativity can be developed in all pupils. This can be done by encouraging pupils to become independent thinkers who can modify, adapt and improve the classroom environment. Teachers should encourage adventure and speculation by creating a positive atmosphere in which there is freedom to reflect, experiment and take risks.

We can look at the creative process in five stages. Each of these stages involves the thinking skills and feelings that make up creativity.

Problem Awareness

This stage requires the ability to recognize that a problem exists, as well as **sensitivity** and **awareness**.

Problem Definition

The second stage involves stating a problem in a meaningful way so that it is easily understood, and therefore requires **imagination**, **curiosity** and **originality**.

Incubation of Ideas

The third stage involves the production of intuitive and original possible answers, before the facts have been checked out. Therefore, this synthesizing process of blending the old with the new requires **fluency, flexibility, originality, elaboration, risk-taking** and **imagination**.

Illumination

The fourth stage requires the **awareness** necessary to provide an instant insight into the solution, often referred to as the 'Aha!' moment.

Evaluation

The final stage requires the **perseverance** to evaluate the validity and full impact of the ideas generated.

Encouragement of creativity requires activities to challenge both 'thinking skills' and 'emotional responses'. This can be done by providing a supportive and stimulating classroom environment that will nurture these processes. On the following page are some ways in which the creative elements of thinking and emotional response can be enhanced.

Overview for the Classroom Teacher

Creativity Catalysts

Creativity Catalysts can be used to generate innovative and original ideas.

Fluency

This initial stage combines the thinking skill of fluency with the emotional responses of imagination, curiosity and originality to generate many different ideas, possibilities and solutions.

Creativity Catalysts:

◆ How many ways … ?
◆ List all the possible uses …
◆ Think of all the problems …
◆ Give as many ideas as you can …
◆ Add to this list …

Flexibility

This stage combines the thinking skill of flexibility with the emotional response of sensitivity to allow the pupil to blend the old with the new, and to see things from many different points of view.

Creativity Catalysts:

◆ What is the relationship between … ?
◆ What would it be like if you were … ?
◆ Categorize …
◆ Rearrange …
◆ Substitute …

Originality

This stage combines the thinking skill of originality with the emotional responses of risk-taking and imagination. It encourages pupils to be inventive and use unique and unexpected approaches.

Creativity Catalysts:

◆ Create …
◆ Design a different way to …
◆ How would you … ?
◆ Invent …
◆ Predict …

Elaboration

This final stage combines the thinking skill of elaboration with the emotional responses of awareness and perseverance. It encourages pupils to expand, develop and add to ideas and materials.

Creativity Catalysts:

◆ Add details to …
◆ Plan …
◆ Expand …
◆ Combine …
◆ Decide …

For more classroom catalysts, use the mnemonic **CREATIVITY** to generate further extension activities.

C Combine: integrate, merge, fuse, brew, synthesize, amalgamate

R Reverse: transpose, invert, transfer, exchange, return, contradict

E Enlarge: magnify, expand, multiply, exaggerate, spread, repeat

A Adapt: suit, conform, modify, alter, emulate, copy, reconcile

T Tinier: minimize, streamline, shrink, squeeze, eliminate, understate

I Instead of, substitute: swap, replace, exchange, alternate, supplant

V Viewpoint change: other eyes, other directions, more optimistically, more pessimistically

I In other sequence: rotate, rearrange, by-pass, vary, submerge, reschedule

T To other uses: change, modify, rework, other values and locations

Y Yes!: Affirm, agree, endorse, concur, approve, consent, ratify, corroborate

Creative Thinking in Literacy

Theme: Poetry

Most bright pupils have a love of words and are captivated by the rhythm and imagery in language.

Poetry is a flexible and creative medium through which pupils are given the opportunity to use their imagination and express their ideas.

The teacher can provide all the pupils with the opportunity to study the structure and forms of poetry, while extending the creative thinking skills of brighter pupils. This can be done by ensuring that the four elements of creative thought are encouraged in the classroom.

Fluency

◆ Have pupils list their favourite poems.

◆ Ask pupils to list different themes for poetry. Examples could be nature, animals or people.

◆ Brainstorm words that could be used for each different theme.

◆ Ask pupils how many different styles of poems they can think of (for example: haikus, limericks, rhyming couplets, free verse).

◆ Have pupils provide examples of the different styles.

◆ Ask pupils which poems make them laugh or make them sad.

◆ Have pupils give examples of similes and metaphors.

Flexibility

◆ Categorize poems under the headings of: rhyming, free verse, nonsense poems and so on.

◆ Ask pupils to think of different ways to group poems (for instance under author, theme or shape).

◆ Have pupils list the ways in which free verse and rhyming poems are different. Then list the ways they are similar.

◆ Ask pupils to nominate their favourite poets and give reasons for their choices.

◆ Have pupils finish similes such as: 'It's as warm as … ' or 'I'm as happy as … '

Originality

◆ Challenge the pupils to create a new form or style of poetry.

◆ Have pupils write a poem about what sunshine would sound like if it had an aural element.

◆ Have pupils work in groups to create a poem that combines words and sounds (for example, a poem about a kettle boiling or someone playing a computer game).

◆ Ask pupils to imagine that they have just interviewed their favourite singer. Instruct them to write the whole interview (questions and answers) in verse.

◆ Have pupils find poems that describe the natural landscape of the UK. Ask them to analyse the types of words and images that are used and then write their own.

Elaboration

◆ Have pupils change 'Twinkle Twinkle Little Star' into a rhyme about a wishing star.

◆ Ask pupils to combine the attributes of a cat, a football and popcorn to write a poem.

◆ Have pupils use their name to write an acrostic poem (that is, where certain letters in each line form a word or words).

◆ Have pupils rewrite a well-known nursery rhyme or poem with the addition of a new character. For example, Old Mother Hubbard's pet lizard.

◆ Have pupils change a happy poem or nursery rhyme into a sad one or vice versa (for example: 'Old King Cole was a sad old soul … ').

◆ Ask pupils to write a round-shape poem and then add new words to it to make it into the shape of a heart.

◆ Write a class poem starting with a funny line like: 'Yuk! Bubblegum in my hair!' Pass it on to the next person and so on, until every person has written one line.

◆ Make a 'Poet-Tree' in your classroom. On the tree pupils can display names, drawings and photos of their favourite poets, their favourite poems, lines, similes and metaphors.

Creative Thinking in Literacy

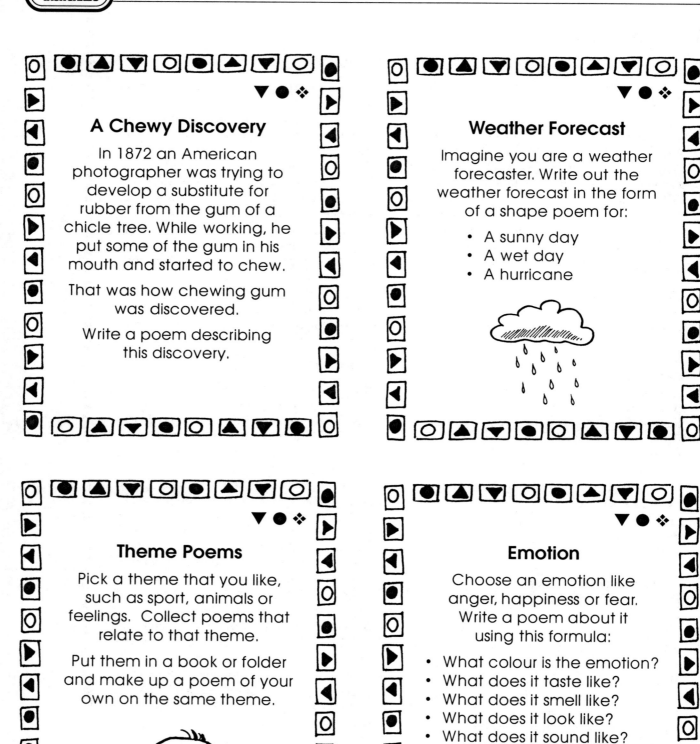

A Chewy Discovery

In 1872 an American photographer was trying to develop a substitute for rubber from the gum of a chicle tree. While working, he put some of the gum in his mouth and started to chew.

That was how chewing gum was discovered.

Write a poem describing this discovery.

Weather Forecast

Imagine you are a weather forecaster. Write out the weather forecast in the form of a shape poem for:

- A sunny day
- A wet day
- A hurricane

Theme Poems

Pick a theme that you like, such as sport, animals or feelings. Collect poems that relate to that theme.

Put them in a book or folder and make up a poem of your own on the same theme.

Emotion

Choose an emotion like anger, happiness or fear. Write a poem about it using this formula:

- What colour is the emotion?
- What does it taste like?
- What does it smell like?
- What does it look like?
- What does it sound like?
- What does it feel like?

Creative Thinking in Literacy

Newsround

Listen to the evening news for two consecutive days.

- Make a list of the main headlines for each day.

- Briefly describe these events.

- Are any of these events reported over the two days?

- Compare the two accounts, how much more information is learned on the second report?

'Phoetry'

Write some 'Phoetry'.

'Phoetry' is a combination of poetry and photography.

Bring in photographs of anything that interests you. Then write poetry that describes actions, impressions, feelings or places represented in the photos.

Someone You Admire

Choose a person you greatly admire.

Make a list of adjectives, similes and metaphors to describe this person. Use these to write a poem dedicated to him/her.

Nonsense Poem

Write a nonsense poem that has in every line:

- A body part and a famous person.

- A kitchen utensil and a dance.

- A colour and a noise.

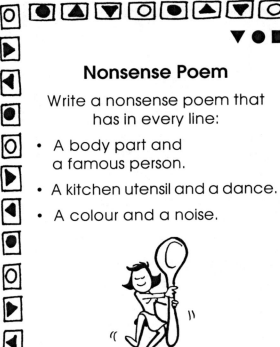

Creative Thinking in Literacy

An Everyday Object

Find three examples of poems written about everyday objects.

Write your own poem about a common object in your home or your classroom.

For example:

An ode to a paper bag.

A limerick about a can of baked beans.

A rhyme about a pair of trainers.

Obituary

Select a poet whose poems you like. Explain why their poetry appeals to you.

Present this information in the form of an obituary. Check the newspaper for examples of different types of obituaries.

Group Poem

In a group of four, each select two lines of poetry that you like the sound of. Write these down and read them out to the rest of the group.

Create your own group poem by using words or even whole lines from these poems.

Give your poem a title and put it up on the wall for others to read.

Epitaph

Research how an epitaph is written.

Write an epitaph about a real or imaginary pet.

Creative Thinking in Literacy

New-age Poem

Write a poem depicting life in the Year 2500.

Present it in an innovative way such as a new language, new form or new structure.

Poetry from Different Cultures

Research poems from two different cultures. You could choose from haiku (Japan), traditional songs/rhymes, American gospel, rap, hip-hop, reggae or African chants.

Compare and contrast the two forms and give reasons for the type you prefer.

Write a poem of your own modelled on one of the types you have chosen.

Ice cream Poem

Imagine you have been asked to write a poem about ice cream.

Think about:

The **form.** Will it be a limerick, rap, nursery rhyme, chant or free verse?

The **structure**. Will it contain similes and metaphors?

Visual **impact**. Will it be a shape poem or a haiku?

Outer-space Poem

The television series Star Trek begins with the words:

'Space, the final frontier. These are the voyages of the Starship Enterprise; its continuing mission to explore strange new worlds; to seek out new life and new civilizations; to boldly go where no one has gone before.'

Write your own preamble to a new television series set in outer space.

Creative Thinking in Maths

Encourage creative thinking in maths by beginning each lesson with a quick challenge to pupils related to the unit of work they are about to study. This will focus the pupils' thinking and encourage active participation in the lesson right from the start. It will also help to create a more positive attitude towards the learning process.

Fluency

Encourage pupils to think about the thinking skills and enquiry processes required for solving problems. Encourage them to brainstorm ideas and come up with a lot of solutions and possibilities. Stimulate discussion with questions like:

◆ What animals can run faster than humans?

◆ The answer is 100. What are 10 questions?

◆ List all the things in the classroom that are shaped like cylinders.

◆ How many different ways of measuring time you can think of?

Flexibility

Expand brainstorming activities by adapting and extending them. Suggestions:

◆ Group the cylinder shapes according to size and weight.

◆ How many other ways can you group these objects?

◆ What reasons can you give for changing the way we measure time?

◆ How many uses can you find for a metre of string?

◆ Find five different objects that are the same size, weight or shape. List all the ways they are different.

◆ What are the similarities between a paper plate and a frisby? Think in terms of size, colour, uses, material, parts and shape.

◆ If you have four coins, how much money could you have?

Originality

Encourage originality by asking open-ended questions, providing pupils with more opportunities to think in the abstract and rewarding creative and innovative solutions. Suggest to the pupils:

◆ Design a maths puzzle for the teacher and others in the class to solve.

◆ Write a story about 5 x 4 = 20 based on your family.

◆ Find a different way to measure a year. Create a new calendar.

◆ Invent a new way of measuring space and weight.

◆ Everyone is walking around backwards. Give three mathematical reasons for this.

Elaboration

Have pupils work in groups or individually to reflect upon the previous three processes. Ask them to look at alternatives, expand on ideas and add more details with activities such as those suggested below:

◆ Make this shape into a different, more complicated form: ⌀

◆ Build a scale model to represent your classroom.

◆ Change a pyramid shape to something different by using BAR (make it **Bigger**, **Add** something and **Replace** something). Draw your new shape.

◆ Draw a maze in the first initial of your name.

◆ Calculate the best area in the school playground where a new swimming pool could be placed. Draw your plan to scale (for example, 1millimetre = 1 metre).

◆ Imagine that you have just won £1000. Describe how you would spend it.

Name:

Management Strategies:
✗ → ●

CREATIVE THINKING
Maths
Worksheet 17

A Model of a Pyramid

You will need:

Scissors, two pieces of card, one copy of a triangle shape to trace around, ruler, tape and glue.

Directions:

1   Trace the shape of the triangle four times onto a piece of card.

2   Cut out all four triangles.

3   Lay the four triangles on your desk with the long edges together and tape the seams.

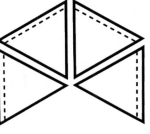

4   Draw a square on your cardboard. Each side of your square must match the short side of your triangle shape in length.

5   Cut out the square.

6   Fold the triangles to a pyramid shape and stand them on the square.

7   Tape them securely.

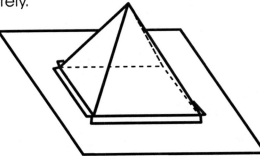

Extension:

Choose a shape like a cube or a cylinder, or something even more challenging, and write out instructions for how to make this shape. Think carefully about each instruction. When you have finished, give your instructions to a friend to follow.

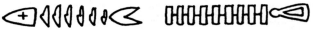

Name:

Rectangle Mobile

Step 1: On a piece of card, draw three rectangles measuring 21cm x 13cm.

Step 2: Mark two of the rectangles 'A' and the third one 'B'.

Step 3: Cut out the rectangles.

Step 4: On both rectangles 'A', measure 3.5cm from the top then draw a dotted line down the centre measuring 14cm as shown below.

Step 5: On rectangle 'B', measure 4cm from the top then draw a dotted line down the centre measuring 17cm as shown below.

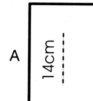

A   14cm   21 cm

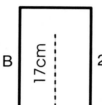

B   17cm   21 cm

Step 6: Cut along the dotted lines.

Step 7: Join rectangles 'A' and 'B' together as shown in the diagram below.

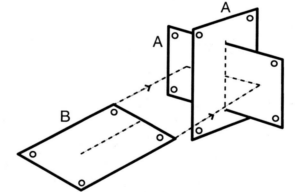

Step 8: With a paper punch, make a hole in each corner of each rectangle.

Step 9: Thread coloured wool through the holes to form triangles.

How many triangles can you form? _____

If you have laced 20 triangles, what is the name of your shape?

_____

Creative Thinking in Maths

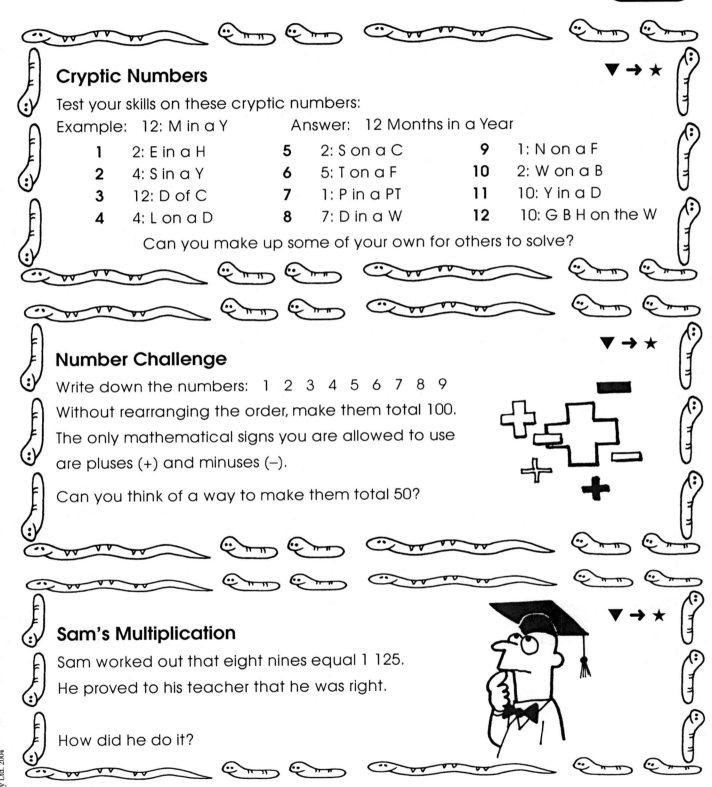

Cryptic Numbers

▼ → ★

Test your skills on these cryptic numbers:

Example: 12: M in a Y   Answer: 12 Months in a Year

1	2: E in a H	5	2: S on a C	9	1: N on a F
2	4: S in a Y	6	5: T on a F	10	2: W on a B
3	12: D of C	7	1: P in a PT	11	10: Y in a D
4	4: L on a D	8	7: D in a W	12	10: G B H on the W

Can you make up some of your own for others to solve?

Number Challenge

▼ → ★

Write down the numbers: 1 2 3 4 5 6 7 8 9

Without rearranging the order, make them total 100.

The only mathematical signs you are allowed to use

are pluses (+) and minuses (–).

Can you think of a way to make them total 50?

Sam's Multiplication

▼ → ★

Sam worked out that eight nines equal 1 125.

He proved to his teacher that he was right.

How did he do it?

Solutions to the above can be found on page 59. Please note that no solution to open-ended questions are provided.

Creative Thinking in Maths

Symbol Sum

→ ★ ▼

Each symbol represents a number in the problem below.

Can you solve the sum?

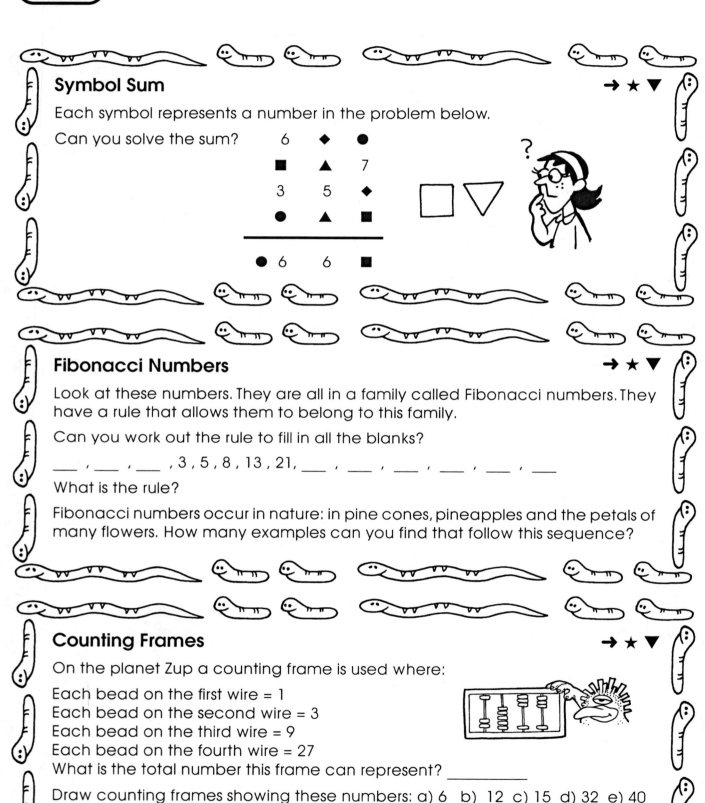

6	◆	●
	■	▲	7
3	5	◆
●	▲	■

▔▔▔▔▔▔▔▔▔

● 6 6 ■

□ ▽

Fibonacci Numbers

→ ★ ▼

Look at these numbers. They are all in a family called Fibonacci numbers. They have a rule that allows them to belong to this family.

Can you work out the rule to fill in all the blanks?

__ , __ , __ , 3 , 5 , 8 , 13 , 21 , __ , __ , __ , __ , __ , __

What is the rule?

Fibonacci numbers occur in nature: in pine cones, pineapples and the petals of many flowers. How many examples can you find that follow this sequence?

Counting Frames

→ ★ ▼

On the planet Zup a counting frame is used where:

Each bead on the first wire = 1
Each bead on the second wire = 3
Each bead on the third wire = 9
Each bead on the fourth wire = 27
What is the total number this frame can represent? _____

Draw counting frames showing these numbers: a) 6 b) 12 c) 15 d) 32 e) 40

Make up your own number systems and give them to others to solve.

Creative Thinking in Science

Theme: Outer Space

Fluency

◆ Brainstorm words about Outer Space.

◆ Ask: 'What is the difference between astronomy and astrology?'

◆ Ask if pupils can list all the planets in our solar system.

◆ Ask: 'What do you know about Mars/Meteorites/UFOs?'

◆ Say: 'The answer is Jupiter. Can you think of 10 questions?'

◆ Pupils list what they know about the Milky Way.

◆ Ask: 'Which planets in our solar system have moons?'

◆ Make a large Concept Map of Space (see page 16 for guidance) and list questions for investigation.

Flexibility

◆ Have pupils think of as many categories as they can in which to group the words about space. Start them off with suggestions such as large and small; near and far.

◆ Ask: 'Why do you think observatories are usually built in remote regions?'

◆ Ask pupils to group the planets in our solar system:
    a) according to size
    b) according to distance from the sun
Have them make a model.

◆ List all the advantages and disadvantages of space travel.

◆ Ask pupils to imagine that Earth was no longer able to sustain human life. List the sort of things which could have happened to create this catastrophe.

◆ Say: 'A manned Space Exploration Flight to Mars has been planned for the Year 2019. Give reasons why you think you should be on board.'

Originality

◆ Ask: 'What does Jupiter sound like?'

◆ Pupils can design an experiment that would test their reaction to weightlessness.

◆ Ask pupils to invent a solar-powered pot-plant waterer.

◆ Say: 'Imagine that you are the first to discover a new planet in our solar system, somewhere beyond the dwarf planet Pluto. What are you going to call it? Describe its shape, size and unique characteristics.'

◆ Encourage pupils to experiment with different ways of launching a miniature UFO using a piece of cardboard, five straws and a rubber band.

◆ Challenge pupils to find a new way to prove that the world is not flat.

Elaboration

◆ Ask pupils to predict how people may change in the future as a result of space travel.

◆ Say: 'Improve on the design of an existing spaceship. Bear in mind that spaceships of the future will be required to carry hundreds of people. They will also have to be very fast and extremely comfortable.'

◆ Pupils can plan 10 questions to ask a visitor from another planet which they consider will tell them all the important facts about life on that planet.

◆ Ask: 'What might the consequences be if Earth's gravity decreased?'

◆ Select a product used in your home and redesign it so it can be used during space travel.

◆ Ask: 'What would happen if the Earth moved 5 000km closer to the sun?'

◆ Pupils could create a model showing the differences between the landscapes on Mars and Earth.

◆ Ask: 'How are other suns the same as ours? How are they different?'

Name:

Solar Systems

On the chart below, all the planets in our solar system are listed in order of their proximity to the sun. Fill in the squares with **YES** or **NO**. Some of the headings have been filled in for you. Use your own ideas for the rest.

Planet	Smaller than Earth	Round	Has moons		
Mercury					
Venus					
Earth					
Mars					
Jupiter					
Saturn					
Uranus					
Neptune					

What do all the planets have in common? _____

_____

In what ways are the planets different? _____

_____

What do Mercury, Venus and Mars have in common? _____

_____

List the planets according to their size. _____

_____

Thinking Strategies for the Successful Classroom, 9–11 Years Old

Brilliant Publications

Name:

Management Strategies:

● ❖

CREATIVE THINKING

Science

Worksheet 20

Space Invention

Invent something unusual that can be used in space.

Suggestions: a feeding machine that can be used in a weightless environment, an alien-greeting robot or a space probe that can be sent out to analyse each new planet you approach.

Describe your invention in the squares set out below.

What is it?	Description of components
How it works	**What it can be used for**
Special features	**Illustration**

Creative Thinking in Humanities

Theme: Pyramids of Egypt

Fluency

◆ Ask: 'Can you name the 'Seven Wonders of the Ancient World'? Where were they located?'

◆ Show locations of the Seven Wonders on a map of the world.

◆ Ask pupils if they know why pyramids were built.

◆ Pupils can list the types of items discovered in the Egyptian pyramids.

◆ Ask pupils to create a word bank of pyramid words.

Flexibility

◆ Say: 'Of all the Seven Wonders of the Ancient World, the only one that remains today is the Great Pyramid. What do you think could be the reason/s for this? How could some of the other structures have been preserved?'

◆ Compare the dimensions of the Great Pyramid to the school building and discuss similarities and differences.

◆ Ask pupils to draw up a list of 10 questions they could ask if they were interviewing one of the citizens of ancient Egypt.

Originality

◆ Ask pupils to brainstorm other uses for pyramids.

◆ Pupils can imagine that they are on an archaeological dig and have made an amazing discovery in one of the Egyptian pyramids. Ask them to describe what it is and why it is so incredible.

◆ Ask pupils to imagine they have found a time capsule from the time of the ancient Egyptians. Have them describe what items are contained within it.

Elaboration

◆ Ask pupils to check library sources or search the Internet to find the styles and intricate patterns of the Egyptian friezes that depicted life in ancient Egypt. Have them create their own frieze to display.

◆ Allow pupils to work in groups to demonstrate how pyramids were built, either by building a model, creating a play or designing a chart. Ask them to improve on the original Egyptian design by making it more efficient.

◆ Pupils can research ancient Egyptian writing. Ask them to invent their own ancient style of writing and write a message that could have been left on the wall of an Egyptian pyramid.

◆ Pupils can research King Tut. Ask them to write a book entitled *The Secrets of Tut's Tomb*. Ask them to imagine what topics this book could cover.

◆ Ask pupils to work in groups to tell the story of the discovery of Tut's Tomb. Have them use music and sound effects to create suspense.

◆ Ask pupils to design a travel brochure about a tour of the Egyptian pyramids.

Name:

Pyramids of Egypt

To the right is a drawing of an Egyptian pyramid.

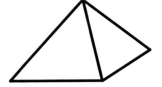

The purpose of the Egyptian pyramid was _____

SUBSTITUTE something: _____

COMBINE it with something else: _____

ADAPT it to make it suitable for another purpose: _____

MODIFY the size: _____

Divide it into **PORTIONS**: _____

ELIMINATE part of it: _____

REVERSE it: _____

After you have written in your ideas for the changes to the Egyptian pyramid, draw your own version. Label all the changes you have made.

My new design is called _____

Its purpose is _____

Name:

Management
Strategies:

Egyptian Writing

If you visit Egypt, you may find some very old writing on some walls. Here are some of the symbols and their meanings:

| reeds | water | boat | sun | good health | food | house | work |

What do you think this says?

My interpretation: _____

_____

_____

_____

Now design your own picture alphabet which tells a story about life in ancient Egypt and the building of the Great Pyramid. When you have finished, give it to a friend to see if they can interpret your story.

My Picture Alphabet Symbols

My Story

Solutions to Worksheets and Task Cards

Answers to puzzles on pages 51 and 52. (Please note that those questions with open-ended responses do not have solutions below.)

Cryptic Numbers

1. 2 Eyes in a Head
2. 4 Seasons in a Year
3. 12 Days of Christmas
4. 4 Legs on a Dog
5. 2 Sides on a Coin
6. 5 Toes on a Foot
7. 1 Partridge in a Pear Tree
8. 7 Days in a Week
9. 1 Nose on a Face
10. 2 Wheels on a Bike
11. 10 Years in a Decade
12. 10 Green Bottles Hanging on the Wall

Number Challenge

$123 + 45 - 67 + 8 - 9 = 100$

Sam's Multiplication

$9 + 9 + 9 + 99 + 999 = 1\ 125$

Symbol Sum

$\blacklozenge = 2$ $\bullet = 1$ $\blacksquare = 4$ $\blacktriangle = 9$

Fibonacci Numbers

1, 1, 2, 3, 5, 8, 13, 21, 34, 55, 89, 144, 233, 377

Counting Frames

162

Research Skills

by **Rosalind Curtis**

Overview for the Classroom Teacher

Research Skills

Research skills are needed by all pupils so that they can analyse and interpret information that is presented to them. Information can be presented to pupils by means of written text, pictures, videos, computer terminal, aural input (listening to speakers, radio, sounds within the environment) and the senses of touch, taste and smell.

Research skills that need to be taught to pupils are:

Questioning Techniques. These help pupils clarify issues, problems and decisions when looking at a topic.

Developing Planning Frameworks. That will assist pupils to access prior knowledge and identify sources of information which will help build further knowledge and understanding.

Gathering Strategies. These help pupils collect and store information for later consideration (for example note taking, identifying main ideas and text clarification).

Sorting Strategies. These help pupils to prioritize and organize information (for example by using retrieval charts and sequencing information).

Synthesizing Skills. These help the pupil to take the original information and reorganize it in order to develop decisions and solutions.

Evaluation. This helps the pupil to determine if the information found is sufficient to support a solution or conclusion.

Reporting Skills. These allow the pupil to translate findings into a persuasive, instructive and effective product (for example in the presentation of a project).

These research skills are best taught within the classroom by means of a **Research Cycle**. This cycle provides pupils with the steps to plan and conduct meaningful research to complete projects, solve problems and make informed decisions.

① Pupils **explore** a variety of sources to gather inform-ation.

⑦ After completion of analysis, pupils will **combine** their findings to create their final project.

② Pupils **identify** inform-ation sources that will contain data to help with their decision.

⑥ Pupils **ask** themselves why this information is important and how it will affect their decision.

③ Once information is found, **decisions** must be made about which data to keep.

⑤ Pupils begin to **analyse** their data by establishing criteria that will help them reach a decision.

④ Pupils **sort** information to enable them to categorize and organize their findings so that analysis can begin.

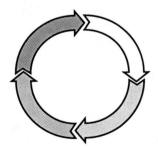

Overview for the Classroom Teacher

The Research Cycle

There are seven steps in the Research Cycle.

1 Questioning

◆ This step identifies the problem that needs solving.

◆ Pupils need to be taught questioning skills that will enable them to identify what data is needed to solve the main problem. It is critical that pupils are encouraged to think laterally and from as many perspectives as possible.

◆ From the questioning process, pupils should be able to identify information they already know and formulate questions to locate information they need to find out.

2 Planning

◆ This step begins to develop information-seeking strategies to help locate answers to all the questions asked.

◆ Pupils need to be introduced to the range of resources which are available, such as books, videos, people, pictures and the Internet.

◆ Pupils need to plan how to organize the information that will be gathered.

3 Gathering

◆ This step enables pupils to clarify the information that has been located.

◆ Pupils need to develop effective note- taking strategies so that the main idea is identified from the information.

◆ Pupils also need to recognize the value of a bibliography so that they may return to an information source if required.

4 Sorting

◆ This step requires pupils to systematically scan the data for relevant information that will contribute to understanding.

◆ Pupils need to classify the gathered information under headings and sub-headings and make generalizations about it.

◆ The data gathered could then be placed into a sequence of events.

5 Synthesizing

◆ This process is like doing a jigsaw puzzle.

◆ Pupils need to arrange and rearrange fragments of information until patterns begin to emerge.

◆ Pupils develop their skills so that they are able to answer questions with understanding, accuracy and detail.

6 Evaluation

◆ When this stage is first reached, early attempts to synthesize information may result in the need for more information to clarify or enhance understanding. If the pupils find that pieces are missing, they will need to begin the cycle again or ask what more is needed to complete their picture.

◆ As the cycle begins again, questioning will become more specific and will lead to more planning and more gathering of information.

◆ When the picture seems to be complete, the pupils can decide that the cycle should finish.

◆ It may be necessary to repeat the cycle and gather more information until the pupils decide that the investigation is complete.

7 Reporting

◆ After the cycle has been completed, it is time to report and share findings. This may take the form of an oral, written or graphic presentation, a debate or any other presentation that pupils may decide upon.

Classroom Design

◆ Ask pupils to work independently, or in mixed-ability or homogeneous groups, as appropriate to the activity.

◆ Provide a variety of resources around the room, including hands-on and extension activities, and learning centres aimed at different levels.

◆ Always give a criteria for marking and a timescale for work to be completed.

Research Skills in Literacy

Theme: Pandas

Questioning

◆ Ask a range of questions about the panda that progressively get more difficult:

> What sort of animal is a panda? W h e r e would I find it? What does it look like? What does it eat? What are some dangers it faces?

◆ Encourage pupils to formulate their own questions.

Planning

◆ Ask pupils to list all that they know about the panda.

◆ Have pupils identify facts or information they would like to find out about the panda (for example, how we can help to preserve its habitat).

◆ Have pupils identify likely sources of information that will assist them.

Gathering

◆ Present written information on pandas and have pupils identify key words by underlining them.

◆ Ask pupils to read books on pandas and take notes.

◆ Ask pupils to suggest words that could be used to search the Internet for information on pandas. Place this list of words on the classroom wall. Develop sub-lists to refine searches. For example: habitat – forests in China, bamboo etc.

Sorting

◆ Ask pupils to group information under headings such as: 'Description', 'Habitat', 'Dangers', 'Habits'.

◆ Pupils can group statements according to common elements and then into 'How are time/sequence relevant?'

Synthesizing

◆ Ask pupils to watch a video related to pandas and devise questions for other pupils to answer.

> Show a picture to the pupils of a forest being cut down. Ask pupils to come up with the types of problems that this could create for the panda.

◆ Allow pupils to access websites such as: **www.WWF.org.uk** and **www.eco-pros. com/ endangeredspecies.htm**. Ask pupils to summarize important facts from these websites. Encourage pupils to prepare an information campaign to be posted on the school notice board.

Evaluating

◆ Pupils can try to convince a friend that pandas are special animals and need to have their habitat preserved.

◆ Ask pupils to write a letter to the local newspaper in support of the 'Save the Panda' fund.

◆ Give pupils some statements about pandas that are incorrect and have the pupils correct them.

Reporting

◆ Have pupils present an oral report explaining why pandas are on the endangered list.

◆ Have pupils work in groups of four to present a play depicting the plight of a panda whose habitat is endangered.

◆ Ask pupils to debate the topic: 'A panda's habitat is more important than urban development'.

Name:

Pandas

Questioning

Make these statements into questions.

Factual

1　Pandas, sheep, dolphins, dogs and humans are all types of mammals.

_____

_____

Inferential

2　With more and more of the panda's habitat being cleared for more families to move into, their numbers are in a forced decline.

_____

_____

Critical

3　I think that we need to stop allowing the panda's habitat to be cleared for housing.

_____

_____

Creative

4　Pandas are very good at climbing trees, but they can also swim.

_____

_____

Factual:

_____

_____

Inferential:

_____

_____

Think of four questions of your own about the panda.

Critical:

_____

_____

Creative:

_____

_____

Name:

Travelling Overseas

Gathering, Sorting, Analysing

1 List the things you would need to organize before leaving the UK to go on an overseas trip.

_____   _____

_____   _____

_____   _____

_____   _____

_____   _____

2 Where would you locate information about the length and cost of an overseas trip?

_____

_____

_____

_____

3 What are some of the problems you could encounter? How would you avoid these problems?

Problem   **How to avoid it**

_____   _____

_____   _____

_____   _____

_____   _____

_____   _____

_____   _____

Research Skills in Literacy

Evaluating

Improving Transport

Choose one form of transport. Improve this form of transport so that it could move more people than it presently does, and would be more comfortable for a long trip.

Draw your new form of transport and describe the improvements you have made.

Alternatives

Find 10 different uses for a helicopter.

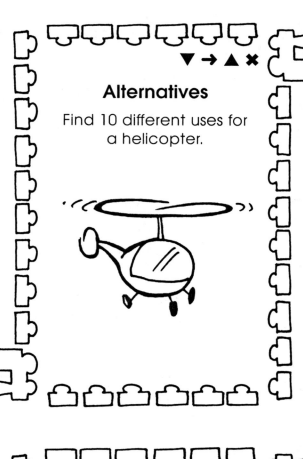

Runaway Train

How could you stop a runaway train by using:

- a fishing net
- a water pistol
- scissors?

Public Transport

Brainstorm solutions for:

'People don't like using public transport.'

Thinking Strategies for the Successful Classroom, 9–11 Year Olds
Brilliant Publications

Research Skills in Literacy

Synthesizing

▼ → ▲

Snow for Sale

Think of some innovative uses for snow.

Design an advertising campaign to sell snow.

FOR SALE

▼ → ▲

Snow Machine

Combine the attributes of a Space Rocket Control Panel and a Lawnmower to design something that can be used in the snow.

▼ → ▲

Explanations

Bright purple snow is falling!

Give five possible explanations for this.

▼ → ▲

Mount Everest

Consider the statement:

'Everyone should be banned from climbing Mount Everest.'

What do you think?

Research Skills in Maths

Theme: Surveys

Questioning

◆ Ensure that pupils understand the language associated with surveys. For example: 'What types of question elicit the desired responses for a survey?'

◆ Ask pupils to look at survey answers represented in different forms (graphs, percentages, statements). Ask them to work with a partner to devise questions for these. For example:
Statement: Most pupils have brown eyes.

　　Question: What colour are your eyes?

◆ Ask pupils to design survey questions relating to preferences that have only two possible answers (for example: 'Is your favourite colour orange or green?').

Planning

◆ Ask pupils to draw a picture for each category of their survey.

◆ Pupils can predict what they think the survey outcome will be.

◆ Have pupils list those people they think they should interview. On what criteria were the people chosen? Will this limit the results of the survey?

Gathering

◆ Conduct surveys on a variety of topics, such as what sort of food pupils eat for their lunch, or what types of cars their parents drive.

◆ Ask pupils to tally responses in a variety of different ways (pictures, tally marks, circles).

Sorting

◆ Pupils can sort their collected data into different categories (for example 'All pupils who like cheese sandwiches.').

◆ If pupils chart their results, have them determine what is included on each axis of a line graph or on each part of a pie chart, (for example: x axis = number who own consoles and y axis = types of consoles, ie x-box, playstation, Wii etc).

Synthesizing

◆ Prepare challenge cards that require pupils to apply maths within real-life situations (for example: 'Which fruit should the school canteen buy more of? Why?').

◆ Ask pupils to interpret information from graphs and to make comparative statements such as: 'There were more wet days in March than dry days.'

◆ Have pupils represent their findings in a variety of graph forms.

Evaluating

◆ Ask pupils to interpret data from a graph that is presented to them.

◆ Let pupils explain why their predictions for survey responses were close to or far from the actual answers.

◆ Have pupils make generalizations about their findings (for example: More people eat cereal than toast for breakfast.).

◆ Ask pupils to decide how they could rephrase a question if it did not provide the desired data.

Reporting

◆ Have pupils summarize and present their findings from surveys that they have conducted.

◆ Encourage pupils to use a variety of means to present their findings visually, such as bar graphs, picture graphs and models.

Name:

Management Strategies:

● ▼ ❖

RESEARCH SKILLS

Maths

Worksheet 25

Survey

You have been asked by the school canteen to find out which food items are the most popular in your class.

Write down four survey questions to find out this information.

Question 1:

_____

_____

_____

Question 2:

_____

_____

_____

Question 3:

_____

_____

_____

Question 4:

_____

_____

_____

Complete the survey with 10 or 20 people and present the information in graph form. You may use a bar graph, pie chart, line graph or picture graph.

Tessellations

Management
Strategies:

● ▼ ❖

Questioning, Analysing,
Synthesizing

Name:

1   On a separate sheet of paper, draw an equilateral triangle with sides of 5cm (see 1).

2   Modify the triangle by cutting into one side and removing a piece (see 2).

3   Transfer this piece to the opposite side of the triangle and re-attach it (see 3).

4   Modify the last side of the triangle by cutting out a small piece. Reattach the cut-out piece to the same side of the triangle (see 4).

5   On a separate sheet of paper make a tessellation using this new shape.

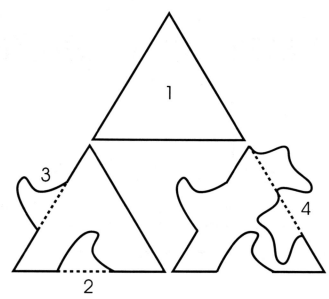

EXTENSION:

Write your own instructions for how to create a tessellation and give them to your friend to follow.

_____

_____

_____

_____

_____

Research Skills in Maths

Evaluating and Synthesizing

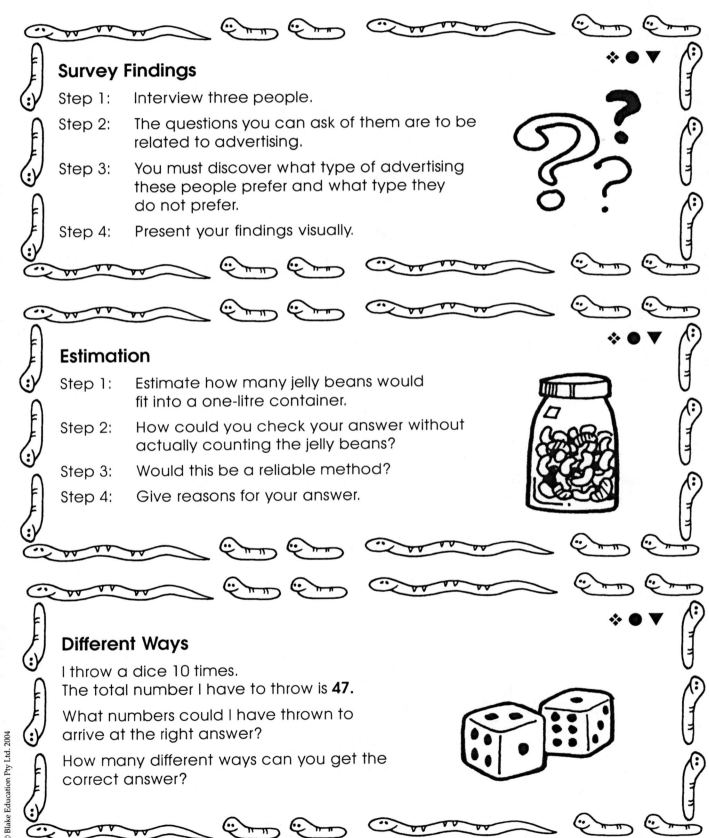

Survey Findings

Step 1:   Interview three people.

Step 2:   The questions you can ask of them are to be related to advertising.

Step 3:   You must discover what type of advertising these people prefer and what type they do not prefer.

Step 4:   Present your findings visually.

Estimation

Step 1:   Estimate how many jelly beans would fit into a one-litre container.

Step 2:   How could you check your answer without actually counting the jelly beans?

Step 3:   Would this be a reliable method?

Step 4:   Give reasons for your answer.

Different Ways

I throw a dice 10 times.
The total number I have to throw is **47**.

What numbers could I have thrown to arrive at the right answer?

How many different ways can you get the correct answer?

Research Skills in Maths

Evaluating and Synthesizing

Measuring an Oval

Step 1: You have to determine the perimeter of an oval. There are no trundle wheels, tape measures or metre rulers available to accurately measure the oval.

Step 2: How would you measure the oval?

Step 3: What would you use as a measuring tool?

Step 4: How would you convert your measurement to metres?

Fun Run

Use a local map for a fun run. The run has to:

- be no longer than 10km
- start and finish at the school
- cross more than five roads.

Draw your fun run detailing landmarks, the streets and directions given to the runners before they begin.

Weighing

Step 1: You have been given a box with measurements of **40**cm long by **60**cm wide and **10**cm high. You need to determine how much it would weigh if you were to fill it with sand. The only measuring tool you have is an old set of kitchen scales that weigh amounts and items up to **750**g. Explain how you would use this set of scales to determine the weight of the full box.

Step 2: What other ways could you think of to determine the weight of the full box of sand?

Research Skills in Science

Theme: Solar System

Questioning

- Ask pupils to write down questions about the solar system that they would like to find answers to such as:

    Which planet looks the brightest in the night sky? Who discovered and named Saturn? Where can we find out more information about our solar system?

- Ask pupils to identify elements needed to sustain life on Earth by asking questions such as:

    What would happen if the sun could not be seen at all? Why do plants need water? How do we rely on plants and animals?

Planning

- Ask pupils to make predictions about what they think would happen if an asteroid hit the Earth.

- Pupils can identify a hypothesis relating to a feature of the solar system that they think would affect Earth in some way (for example: 'If the night sky was cloudy, how would this have affected the navigation of sailing ships in the 19th century?').

Gathering

- Encourage pupils to track the paths of stars and planets over a period of time.

- Ask pupils to consult past records of planets or star positions for a specific time each year, and compare it with the present position. Record the date, season and month. Compare and contrast results.

- Ask pupils to identify scientific concepts of observation, hypothesizing and generalizing relating to different elements of the solar system.

    a) Observation: watching and recording phases of the moon.

    b) Hypothesizing: the planets will return to the same position in the sky at set intervals.

    c) Generalizing: comets have set paths that they follow around the sun, as do planets.

Sorting

- Ask pupils to sort various items according to different attributes (for example, planets could be sorted into large and small).

- Encourage pupils to discuss their observations in terms of cause and effect (for example, the moon circling the Earth determines our tides).

- Ask pupils to categorize elements for sustaining life into human-controlled and nature-controlled elements.

- Ask pupils to explain (in the correct sequence) the procedures necessary to carry out an experiment such as, investigating the effect of gravity on satellites orbiting the Earth.

Synthesizing

- Pupils can design and build models of our own and a 'new' solar system.

- Ask pupils to write a 'letter to the Editor' about the effects of space junk on our solar system.

- Using the laws of probability and past records, have pupils predict the path of Halley's Comet in 2056.

Evaluating

- Ask pupils to think of ways to maintain life after a nuclear holocaust or when colonizing another planet.

- Ask pupils to explain why their new system could sustain life.

- Let pupils describe the attributes of planets that make them belong to a specific grouping (for example, planets with moons).

Reporting

- Have a Science Fest where pupils exhibit a project relating to our solar system that they have devised and carried out.

Name:

Solar System

TASK 1: Work in groups of four to become experts on one of the following:

moon	satellite	black hole
sun	planet	comet
asteroid	star constellation	

Each member of the group must write down the information that is gathered. Use this space to make your notes.

My group became an expert on: _____

Key Facts:

_____   _____

_____   _____

_____   _____

_____   _____

TASK 2: Join with an expert from each of the other groups. Give your information about your member of the solar system.

TASK 3: Within your new group, combine all the objects you have described to form a new solar system. Give the system a name. Make a sketch of what the solar system would look like.

TASK 4: Make a 3D display your new system. Label all parts of your solar system. Write an explanation of how each part of the solar system interacts with the other parts and attach it to your display.

Research Skills in Humanities

Theme: Survival

Questioning

◆ Ask pupils to identify what they already know about survival.

◆ Prepare questions for pupils to answer which will encourage them to think about survival skills. For example:

- What do I need to survive? (Factual)

- What does survival mean? (Factual)

- How do I ensure that I have everything I need to survive? (Inferential)

- If I had to do without something to survive, what would it be? (Critical)

- If I could add another element to my needs for survival, what would it be? (Creative)

Planning

◆ List resources that could be used to find information about survival:

- Non-fiction books relating to the human body or survival techniques.

- Fiction books such as *Robinson Crusoe* or *Swiss Family Robinson*.

- The Internet.

- Biographies of people who have survived after aeroplane crashes or shipwrecks.

◆ Ask pupils to draw a diagram to help with their storing of information.

◆ Ask pupils to identify what they need to find out about survival.

Gathering

◆ Get pupils to read extracts from fiction that detail how people survived after shipwrecks or being lost in the wilderness.

◆ Pupils can identify key words from texts that relate to survival. This could form the basis of a survival handbook.

◆ Show videos such as *Swiss Family Robinson*. Ask pupils to write down ways that the family survived.

Sorting

◆ Ask pupils to compile, using their notes on *Swiss Family Robinson*, lists of things that you can use from nature to survive and artificial things that have been developed by people to survive.

◆ Pupils can identify examples of cause and effect (for example: 'The storm caused the ship to sink. The effect was being isolated on a tropical island.').

Synthesizing

◆ Ask the pupils to think of all the ways the family could use a piece of rope, a sheet and a bucket to help them gather food and retrieve things from the ship.

◆ Ask pupils to think of things they would need to do to make life bearable until a rescue ship arrived.

Evaluating

◆ Pupils list three people they would like to be shipwrecked with and give reasons for their choices.

◆ Ask pupils to list things they would need to retrieve from the ship to help in their survival.

Reporting

◆ Show pupils how to keep a log of their stay on the island detailing how they spent their time.

◆ Ask pupils to role-play their rescue.

◆ Encourage pupils to write a newspaper article detailing the rescue.

Name:

Survival Skills

Gathering, Synthesizing,
Evaluating

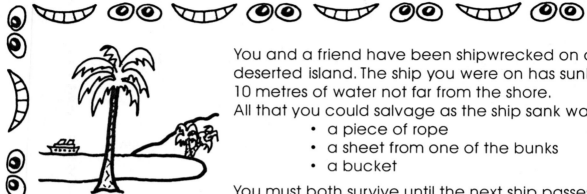

You and a friend have been shipwrecked on a deserted island. The ship you were on has sunk in 10 metres of water not far from the shore.
All that you could salvage as the ship sank was:

- a piece of rope
- a sheet from one of the bunks
- a bucket

You must both survive until the next ship passes in 30 days.

How would these items help you survive?

_____

_____

_____

Give examples of challenges or dangers that you might face.

_____

_____

_____

Describe what you would do to survive.

_____

_____

_____

Invent an implement that would help you to attract the attention of the passing ship. Describe and illustrate how this will help you.

_____

_____

_____

Thinking Strategies for the Successful Classroom, 9–11 Year Olds   Brilliant Publications

Research Skills in Creative Arts

Theme: Designing an Exhibit for the Local Museum

Questioning

◆ Ask the question: 'How many different types of museums are there?'

◆ Ask pupils to list what they would find at a museum.

◆ Get pupils to clarify vocabulary such as, 'artefacts', 'hieroglyphs', 'excavations'.

◆ Ask pupils to identify things they would like to know about museums and displays:

- Where is my nearest museum?

- What items would be suitable to display at this museum?

- Who could I talk to about setting up a display?

- What steps do I need to take to set up a display?

Planning

◆ Ask pupils to plan what they would like to exhibit.

◆ Ask pupils to list resources that could be used to locate information for designing and planning their exhibit (for example: the Internet, encyclopedias, local museum).

◆ Pupils can draw up a list of questions for data they need to locate.

◆ Model a mind map, then have pupils devise their own, using the questions they have listed.

◆ Ask pupils to think about time-lines for the items they are exhibiting.

Gathering

◆ Pupils could visit a local museum to observe ways that exhibits are presented.

◆ Ask pupils to identify indicators for determining the age of artefacts from videos and written texts.

◆ Ask pupils to write down key facts about the world of 2 000 years ago.

Sorting

◆ Have pupils organize their data about artefacts into a time-line.

◆ Ask pupils to list the things that would have been used 2 000 years ago, such as clay pots, statues and gold jewellery.

◆ Have pupils sort information about artefacts into various categories (for example: 'Household Items' or 'Valuable Items').

Synthesizing

◆ Have pupils write a description of an exhibit they saw at the museum.

◆ Ask pupils to identify problems that could arise with their exhibit.

◆ Have pupils design a poster advertising the exhibition.

Evaluating

◆ Ask pupils to evaluate an exhibition they have seen.

◆ Pupils can design the layout for their exhibit, showing where each item will be placed.

◆ Ask pupils to design the display according to for example, chronological order, materials from which artefacts were made or places where artefacts were found. Ask them to explain their reason for choosing this style of display.

Reporting

◆ Ask pupils to make a model of their display.

◆ Ask pupils to write an article for the newspaper reporting on the display.

RESEARCH SKILLS

Creative Arts

Worksheet 29

Name:

Management Strategies:

Gathering, Sorting, Evaluating

Designing an Exhibition

You have been asked to design a new exhibit for the local museum containing artefacts found during the excavations of a city believed to be over 2 000 years old. How would you choose what to display and the information provided for visitors?

Use this sheet to jot down your ideas and to begin your preliminary sketches of the exhibit. Include some drawings of artefacts that will be on display.

List of artefacts chosen for display	Information about the artefacts

Plan of display

 Thinking Strategies for the Successful Classroom, 9–11 Year Olds   Brilliant Publications

This page may be photocopied for use by the purchasing institution only.

© Blake Education Pty Ltd 2004

Make Your Own Task Cards

Questioning Skills and Brainstorming

by **Rosalind Curtis**

Overview for the Classroom Teacher

Questioning Skills and Brainstorming

Generally speaking, 30% of class time is taken up in questioning (that is about 100 questions per hour). In most classrooms, 85% of questions are asked by the teacher, and 90% of those do no more than demand simple recall by the pupils! Therefore, teachers should aim to use more open-ended and divergent questions to improve pupils' creative-thinking and problem-solving abilities.

Questioning Guidelines for the Teacher:

1. Maintain a high level of enthusiasm.

2. Accept that individual differences in pupils will determine how, what, how much and how fast learning occurs.

3. Encourage divergent thinking.

4. Avoid all forms of 'put-downs'. Be positive! Say: 'Great!', 'Good try!', 'Tell me more!', 'I've never thought of it like that!'

5. Try to minimize 'Who?', 'What?' or 'Where?' and maximize 'Why?' and 'How?'

Bloom's Taxonomy emphasizes the idea that, with brighter pupils, more time should be devoted to the higher-level activities and objectives. *Knowledge* and *Comprehension* deal with facts, figures, definitions and rules, which all pupils need to know. However, teachers should encourage the brighter pupils (who will generally grasp new information quickly and comprehend more rapidly) to:

◆ *Apply* this knowledge;

◆ *Analyse* components, relationships and hypotheses;

◆ *Synthesize* these components into creative solutions, plans and theories;

◆ *Evaluate* the accuracy, value and efficiency of alternative ideas or actions.

Examples of questions that help to apply knowledge:

When did ... ?

Can you list ... ?

Which action/event was the cause of ... ?

Can you give an example of ... ?

How would you have ... ?

Why was ... ?

Examples of questions that help to analyse knowledge:

Why did ... do this?

Can you sequence ... ?

Examples of questions that help to synthesize knowledge:

How would this situation have changed if ... ?

What if the 'bears' had been 'monkeys'?

Examples of questions that help to evaluate the knowledge:

How could ... have been improved?

Who do you think has the strongest character? Why?

Overview for the Classroom Teacher

Brainstorming

Another questioning technique that encourages creative thinking is **brainstorming.**

The aim of brainstorming is to develop a safe, non-judgemental setting where all pupils feel confident and eager to participate in the lesson.

It was Alex Osborn who identified some valuable conditions and rules for brainstorming. The main principle is *deferred judgement*. This means that idea evaluation is postponed until later. Osborn stressed that any kind of criticism or evaluation interferes with the generation of imaginative ideas, simply because it is very difficult to do both at the same time.

It is important for the teacher to remind the pupils of the basic rules of brainstorming:

1. No criticism is allowed, no matter how irrelevant or preposterous the responses may appear to be.

2. Quantity of ideas is required. The more ideas you have, the more likely it is that you will have motivated all pupils to contribute, and thus it is more likely that you will find good solutions.

3. Accept and record all answers. To begin with, it is perhaps easier for the teacher to be the scribe, but when brainstorming is a regular feature of the class's activities, pupils can record responses.

4. Eliminate any stiffness or inflexibility. Be open to alternatives.

5. If responses slacken off, add your own. The teacher's role is to keep urging: 'What else could we do?' 'Who else has an idea?' The teacher may even specifically direct questions to a group of quieter pupils.

6. Link ideas wherever possible. Ask questions such as: 'How can we express this more clearly?' 'Could we improve this one?' 'What if we put these three ideas together?'

7. Encourage fantasy, imagination and lateral thinking.

8. Encourage co-operative work among pupils.

9. If there were a school problem (for example, the sudden appearance of graffiti in the school playground), the pupils could be given 24 hours' notice so that *all* have an opportunity to discuss this at home and be prepared to brainstorm a solution for the next day. Brighter pupils soon learn to organize and lead group brainstorming sessions.

Some variations of brainstorming are:

Reverse Brainstorming: This technique quickly points out what is currently being done incorrectly and implicitly suggests specific solutions (for example: 'How can we *increase* vandalism?').

'Stop and Go' Brainstorming: Short periods of approximately 6–8 minutes of brainstorming are interspersed with evaluation. The evaluation sheets help keep the group on target by selecting the most profitable directions to pursue.

Phillips 66: This is a technique using groups of six. Pupils brainstorm for six minutes and then a member of each group reports the best, or all, ideas to the larger group.

Questioning Skills and Brainstorming in Literacy

Theme: Heroes and Heroines

Knowledge

◆ Explain that the word 'hero' will be used to refer to both males and females.

◆ Brainstorm: 'What makes a person a hero?'

◆ Ask pupils: 'Can you write a definition of a hero?'

◆ Ask the questions: 'Are there any particular occupations from which 'heroes' emerge? Why do you think this is so?'

Comprehension

Ask questions such as:

◆ Can you name any heroes? What did these people do to become heroes?

◆ Do all heroes fit a certain physical stereotype? For example, are they all tall, strong and athletic?

◆ Does a hero have to be a human being? Why? Why not?

◆ Challenge pupils to think of a sequence of questions to determine if someone/ something is a hero.

Application

Brainstorm:

◆ Who were some heroes from history? (Include examples from different areas, such as Florence Nightingale, Mary Seacole and Jesse Owens.)

◆ Why are these people remembered as heroes?

◆ Who are some heroes from fictional stories or movies? Why are they considered heroes?

◆ Can you think of some heroes from recent news stories? What made them heroes?

◆ Do you think you have the qualities to be a hero? Why/Why not?

Analysis

◆ Have the pupils list all the ways that people in the following occupations could be heroes:

a) teachers   b) doctors

c) plumbers   d) nurses

e) bank cashiers   f) pupils

g) bus drivers

◆ Brainstorm: 'Why are soldiers often thought of as heroes? Why are medals or commendations given to many of them?'

Synthesis

◆ Have the pupils work in groups of three or four to list all the ways that they could become a hero.

◆ Say: 'If you were able to interview one of the heroes you have named, who would you choose? Why? List five questions you would like to ask them.'

◆ Ask: 'Do you think that heroes are ever afraid? Why? Why not? If yes, then what might they be afraid of?'

Evaluation

◆ Pose the question: 'What is admired most about a hero?'

◆ Ask: 'How can we best let a person know if we think they are a hero?'

◆ Allow the pupils to work in small groups of four or five, to list the 10 most important qualities they think a hero should possess. Then they can look again at the questions they designed for 'Comprehension' to determine if someone/something was a hero. Are the questions sufficient?

◆ Ask pupils to write a report about someone they know personally who might be considered a hero.

Questioning Skills and Brainstorming in Literacy

Knowledge, Comprehension, Application, Analysis

Nicknames

What are the nicknames of these famous people? Why do you think they were given them?

Florence Nightingale

Margaret Thatcher

The Duke of Wellington

Martin Luther King, Jnr.

Favourite Heroes

Work with a partner to list your 10 favourite heroes.

State which field they are from and why you chose them.

Humanitarian Heroes

Work in groups of 3 or 4. Choose one of these humanitarian heroes to research and write a report that highlights some of the ways they have helped people.

Mother Teresa
Mahatma Gandhi
Albert Schweitzer
William Wilberforce

Book Heroes

Name some of the heroes created by these writers:

J R R Tolkein
Eoin Colfer
Louis Sachar
Enid Blyton
J K Rowling

Draw your favourite book hero and add your illustration to a class 'Book Heroes Wall of Fame.'

Questioning Skills and Brainstorming in Literacy

Analysis, Synthesis, Evaluation

Non-Human Hero

Suggest a scenario where a non-human becomes a hero.

Cartoon Hero

Who is your favourite cartoon hero?

Draw him/her in action.

My Hero

From all the people you have ever known, read about or heard about, choose one person who impresses you most.

Write a haiku or limerick about this person.

My Turn to Be a Hero

Write the letters **A–Z** down one side of your page. For each letter, think of a situation in which you could become a hero (for example: **A**valanche – I could help to rescue someone from beneath the snow).

Name:

Heroes

Synthesis

Imagine you have the opportunity to become a hero.

Choose one of these scenarios:
- a fire
- an accident
- a storm

Display your heroic feats in this cartoon strip.

Thinking Strategies for the Successful Classroom, 9–11 Year Olds   Brilliant Publications

Name:

Management Strategies:

▼ ✳ ▲

Analysis, Synthesis, Evaluation

QUESTION/ BRAINSTORM

Literacy

Worksheet 31

Heroes

What can you find out about each of these heroes?

Write a short description of their accomplishments, and select one other hero in their field of excellence.

Medicine

Louis Pasteur

_____
_____
_____
_____
_____
_____
_____
_____

Another hero is:

Sport

Jonny Wilkinson

_____
_____
_____
_____
_____
_____
_____
_____

Another hero is:

Defence Forces

Lord Nelson

_____
_____
_____
_____
_____
_____
_____
_____

Another hero is:

Humanitarian

Martin Luther King

_____
_____
_____
_____
_____
_____
_____
_____

Another hero is:

Writing

Anne Frank

_____
_____
_____
_____
_____
_____
_____
_____

Another hero is:

Music

Ray Charles

_____
_____
_____
_____
_____
_____
_____
_____

Another hero is:

Questioning Skills and Brainstorming in Maths

Theme: Time

Knowledge

◆ Brainstorm: 'Why do people need to know the time of day/week/month/year?'

◆ Brainstorm different ways of telling the time (for example, 7.15 could also be expressed as:

    a) 15 minutes past 7

    b) a quarter past seven

    c) 07.15(am) or 19.15(pm)

◆ Find out what pupils know about the new Internet time.

Comprehension

◆ Ask pupils to research how our ancestors told the time of day and year (for example, the sun dial). Ask them if some people still use these methods.

◆ Ask the questions: 'When did the first clocks appear? What form did these early clocks take?'

◆ Ask: 'When were the first watches invented?'

◆ Get pupils to describe how they think clocks or digital watches work.

Application

◆ Give pupils copies of various timetables (bus, train, aeroplane) and ask questions about them (for example: 'If you lived in Glasgow and wanted to arrive in Manchester in time for a meeting at 1pm on Wednesday, which flight would you have to catch?'

◆ Ask: 'What are some occasions when people depend on knowing the correct time?'

◆ Provide pupils with a cardboard replica of an ordinary clockface and have them fill in a second circle of numbers to produce a 24-hour clockface.

◆ Ask pupils where 24-hour time is commonly used? Ask them to provide reasons for this.

◆ Have each pupil select a number between 0 and 99. Ask them to create a time-line of events that occurred in that year of each century. For example if they select '60', they could choose: 1960 – John F. Kennedy became President of the United States; 1860 – Lister pioneered work on antiseptic surgery; 1760 – George III became King of England. Make

sure that each pupil chooses a different number, and display the results of their work around the classroom.

Analysis

◆ Ask pupils to list as many early 'time-tellers' as they can. Ask: 'In what ways were these early timepieces not always satisfactory?'

◆ Challenge pupils to name as many present-day 'time indicators' as they can. Ask them to select those used for very short as well as very long time spans.

◆ Ask: 'Why do we need such a variety of instruments to tell the time?'

◆ Pupils can research where these time indicators can be found (for example: in a family home or in a special establishment).

Synthesis

Ask questions about Time Zones for pupils to investigate:

◆ Why is the time in London different from the time in Berlin or New York?

◆ When we watch sports such as tennis or cricket being televised live from Australia, why do we have to watch them at night, if they are being played during the day?

◆ Where is the International Date Line? What is its importance?

◆ What is Greenwich Mean Time? Where is Greenwich?

Evaluation

◆ Investigate pupils' knowledge and opinions about British Summer Time by asking:

    What is British Summer Time? When do we use it? Why do we use it? Do you think it is a good or bad thing? Why?

◆ Ask pupils to give reasons for why speed limits are placed on road traffic.

◆ Ask: 'What is meant by the "Speed of Light" and the "Speed of Sound"?'

◆ Have pupils compare these two speeds with:

    - the speed at which you can run 50 metres

    - the speed at which Mum or Dad drives the car to the shopping centre.

Questioning Skills and Brainstorming in Maths

Comprehension, Application, Analysis

Estimation

Estimate how long it would take to do each of the following, and then record the actual time taken:

Print your first name.

Count out £1 in 5 pence pieces.

Walk 50 metres.

Tie your shoelaces.

Run around the school.

Hand out a book to each class member.

Calculation

How many days, hours and minutes from now until:

Christmas Day?

Mothering Sunday?

You turn 14?

Time Development

What effect did each of the following people have on the development of accurate timekeeping?

• Julius Caesar

• Pope Gregory XIII

• John Harrison

Graphing

Work with a partner. Time each other doing the following activities over 100 metres and show your results in graph form. Use line, bar, pie or picture graphs.

• Running

• Walking

• Skipping

• Walking backwards

Questioning Skills and Brainstorming in Maths

Analysis, Synthesis, Evaluation

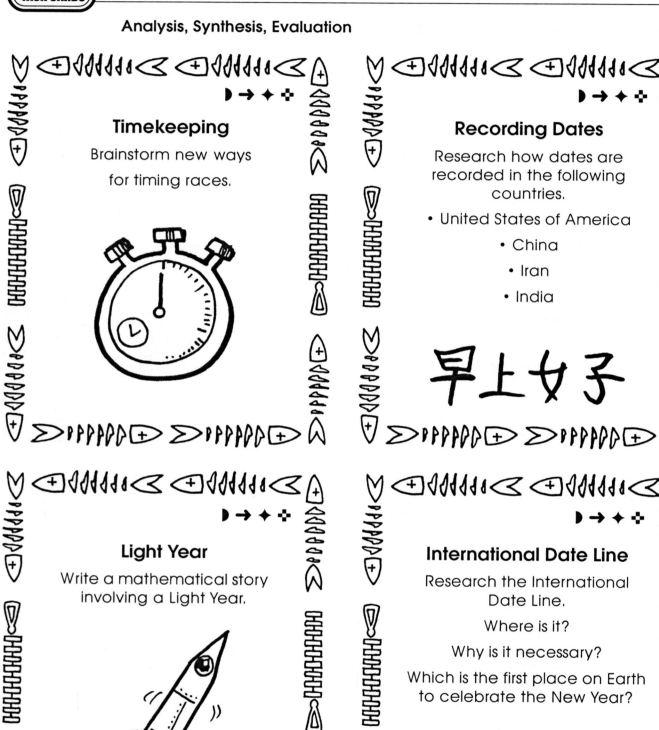

Timekeeping

Brainstorm new ways
for timing races.

Recording Dates

Research how dates are
recorded in the following
countries.

- United States of America
  - China
  - Iran
  - India

早上女子

Light Year

Write a mathematical story
involving a Light Year.

International Date Line

Research the International
Date Line.

Where is it?

Why is it necessary?

Which is the first place on Earth
to celebrate the New Year?

Thinking Strategies for the Successful Classroom, 9–11 Year Olds   Brilliant Publications

Name: _____

Management
Strategies:

▼ → ✲

QUESTION/
BRAINSTORM
Maths
Worksheet 32

Time Research Tasks

Comprehension,
Application, Analysis

Illustrate the following timepieces and explain how each one operates.

Sundial	Clepsydra

Description: _____

_____

_____

_____

Description: _____

_____

_____

_____

Candle	Caesium Atomic Clock

Description: _____

_____

_____

_____

Description: _____

_____

_____

_____

Name:

Time Tasks

Analysis, Synthesis,
Evaluation

TASK 1: Explain the meaning of these time words:

Millennium _____

Olympiad _____

Lunar month _____

Calendar month _____

BC _____

Solstice _____

Equinox _____

TASK 2: Complete this Pie Chart to indicate how your day is spent at school. Show all your subjects, lunch and breaktimes, and the time each one takes.

TASK 3: Draw a Pie Chart showing how your ideal day would be spent.

Thinking Strategies for the Successful Classroom, 9–11 Year Olds

Brilliant Publications

Questioning Skills and Brainstorming in Science

Theme: Food

Knowledge

Brainstorm:

◆ What is food?

◆ Who needs food?

◆ Why do we all need food?

◆ What is your favourite food? (Record all responses and use this information for drawing up bar graphs, picture graphs or pie charts.)

Comprehension

Brainstorm:

◆ Why do we need variety in the food we eat?

◆ Why is breakfast known as 'the most important meal of the day'?

◆ What is a dietitian?

Application

◆ Ask each member of the class to keep a Daily Diary recording all of the food they consume, over a period of one week.

◆ Invite a dietitian to your school to speak to your class or year group about:

- The food they should be eating

- The food they should be reducing in their intake

- Why they should eat more of some foods and less of others

- How often they should eat

Analysis

◆ Ask pupils to refer to the Daily Diary activity and divide their foods into ones that they should eat more of (eg apples) and ones that they should eat less of (eg crisps)

◆ Brainstorm what pupils now understand to be the notion of a 'balanced diet'. Have pupils design a list of 10 questions to determine if someone has a balanced diet.

◆ Get the pupils to draw up a list of the five main food groups and give examples of common foods in each group.

◆ Brainstorm: 'What does the old saying "You are what you eat" mean?'

◆ Analyse the types of foods sold from the school canteen. Draw up a pie graph of the most popular foods.

Synthesis

◆ Ask pupils to think of ways that they could improve the quality of their daily food intake.

◆ Allow pupils to work in groups to discuss and list the food advertisements that have influenced them most. Then ask them to design their own food advertisement.

◆ Encourage pupils to imagine that they are dietitians, then ask them to devise answers to questions they could be asked by clients. For example:

- What is the best way for me to lose weight?

- If I want to gain weight, should I just eat more?

- Why are liquids such an important part of a food plan?

Evaluation

◆ Ask pupils to evaluate why food needs of adolescents are different from those of adults and different again from those of the elderly.

◆ Ask: 'Why do you think most children don't like vegetables? Can you think of a solution to this problem?'

◆ Encourage pupils to create a 'Healthy Eating' display for the classroom, school library or assembly hall.

Name:

Planning a Dinner Menu

TASK 1: How many of your favourite foods originated in another country? Complete this table.

Country	Name of Dish	Main Ingredients	Score /10
Italy			
Spain			
China			
India			

TASK 2: On a separate sheet of paper, record your family's preferences for each country.

Use this information to plan a dinner menu for your family. Remember to include all five food groups.

Print the menu for your Special Dinner.

Special Family Menu

Starter/Soup:

Main Course:

Dessert:

Name:

Management Strategies:

◗ ✦ ★

Analysis, Synthesis, Evaluation

Lunch Special

TASK 1: Organize a 'Lunch Special' for your school canteen. Make sure that as well as being tasty it is also healthy.

Describe and illustrate your meal in the box below.

Name of Lunch Special:	Illustration
Description:	

TASK 2: Design and produce an advertising poster for your Lunch Special.

Questioning Skills and Brainstorming in Humanities

Theme: Disasters Around the World

Knowledge

Involve the class in a discussion on 'disasters'. Give the class five minutes to think up their own questions about disasters. Ask one pupil to read a question to the class to start the discussion and then others take turns, as it progresses. Some typical discussion questions may include:

◆ Have you ever seen a disaster? Can you describe to the class what happened?

◆ How would you describe a disaster?

◆ What are some recent disasters?

◆ Where did these disasters take place?

◆ What are some other major disasters that have taken place throughout time?

◆ Would an aeroplane crash be classed as a disaster? Why? Why not?

◆ What is the 'Richter Scale'?

Comprehension

Check pupils' understanding of disasters with questions such as:

◆ What sort of damage have some of the disasters we have already discussed caused to property and/or to people?

◆ Have you ever experienced a disaster or even a 'mini-disaster'?

◆ What was it like? How did you feel during this experience?

Application

◆ Organize a visit to your nearest Science Centre to provide pupils with an insight into earthquake movement.

◆ Ask the question: 'Can you predict or imagine what this classroom might look like if we were involved in an earthquake or a hurricane?'

◆ Ask: 'What would the school and playground be like if they had been in the path of a forest fire?'

◆ Ask the pupils to find out about the San Andreas Fault. Ask them to find out where it is and why it is so well known.

Analysis

◆ Have pupils brainstorm the difference between a 'natural' and a 'people-made' disaster.

◆ Ask pupils to nominate recent disasters which fit into these categories.

◆ Ask: 'Which type of disaster do you think would be more frightening? Why?'

◆ Allow pupils to work in small groups to investigate any patterns emerging from the places where natural disasters have occurred.

◆ Ask pupils to research the theory of 'Plate Tectonics'.

Synthesis

◆ Allow pupils to work in groups to suggest ways in which the number and severity of people-made disasters could be reduced.

◆ Pupils can brainstorm all organizations whose main function is to develop ways to avoid disasters or at least reduce their effects on communities.

◆ Ask: 'Which country leads the world in forecasting the occurrence of earthquakes? Why do you think this is so?'

Evaluation

◆ Ask: 'How and when is a tragic event classified as a disaster?'

◆ Have pupils work in small groups to brainstorm ways in which they could minimize the outcomes of some of these disasters.

◆ Ask: 'What are some occupations in which it is crucial to have up-to-date knowledge of weather forecasts? Why?'

Questioning Skills and Brainstorming in Humanities

Knowledge, Application, Analysis

Map Work

On a map of the world, name and indicate the positions of:

- active volcanoes
- recent earthquake zones
- tornado or hurricane areas

Models

Work in groups of three or four. Choose one of the following disasters for a five-minute oral presentation to the class.

You can use photographs, diagrams or models.

- Earthquakes
- Hurricanes
- Volcanic Eruptions
- Landslides/Avalanches

Met Office

Find out from the Met Office how their work helps to minimize the effects of:

Hail

Heat waves

High winds

Flooding

Plagues and Pests

In pairs, brainstorm the following:

What was the Black Plague?

What diseases are caused by mosquitoes?

What damage is done by locusts?

Then research to see if you were correct.

QUESTION/
BRAINSTORM

Humanities

Worksheet 36

Name:

**Management
Strategies:**

▼ ◗ →
✶ ✤ ✖

Disasters Around the World

Analysis,
Synthesis, Evaluation

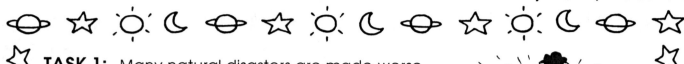

TASK 1: Many natural disasters are made worse
by human activity.

Give an example for each one of these:

Disaster	Human Activity
Floods	
Forest fires	
Landslides	
Famine	
Earthquakes	

TASK 2: Illustrate two recent people-made disasters.

Brainstorm ways the disaster could have been avoided or the
damage reduced.

1:	2:
Ways to Avoid Disaster 1	**Ways to Avoid Disaster 2**
_____	_____
_____	_____
_____	_____
_____	_____

Make Your Own Task Cards

Renzulli's Enrichment Triad

by **Fay Holbert**

Thinking Strategies for the Successful Classroom, 9–11 Year Olds

Brilliant Publications

Overview for the Classroom Teacher

Introduction to Renzulli's Enrichment Triad Model

The Enrichment Triad Model was devised by Joseph Renzulli in 1983 as a framework to provide pupils with the skills to carry out their own research investigations. Renzulli believes that all pupils should be given the opportunity to develop higher-order thinking skills and pursue enriched high-end learning.

When implementing the Enrichment Triad Model in the classroom, the teacher's priority is the development of independence and encouragement of self-directed learning. The open-endedness of this model gives pupils the freedom to make choices about topics, resources and manner of presentation. Teachers will also find a freedom in structure that allows them to guide their pupils through investigations and projects step by step, while still being able to change the process to suit the needs of individual pupils.

The Three Types of Activities

There are three types of activities within the Triad Model. They are:

Type I – exploratory experiences. Pupils' interests are identified. Pupils are given the opportunity to explore something new and extend their learning within a familiar topic.

Type II – group training activities. These activities promote the development of thinking and feeling processes with a major focus on advanced levels of thinking. These activities provide pupils with the necessary skills to carry out individual and small group investigations and include:

- Creative and critical-thinking skills
- Decision making
- Problem solving
- Communication skills
- Research skills

These activities develop 'learning how to learn' skills. They focus on:

- Improving creativity
- Research techniques
- How to use different types of equipment

Type III – individual and/or small-group investigations of real issues. Pupils use appropriate methods of research and inquiry and develop management plans to aid in completion of the investigation.

Type I and II enrichment activities provide the basic skills needed for pupils to carry out their own or group investigations. Type III enrichment activities require a high level of commitment from the pupils and actively engage them in the learning process by expecting them to add new knowledge, ideas or products to a field of study. (**Note:** ensure that pupils have participated in Type I and Type II activities before embarking on a Type III activity.)

All three types of enrichment activities are interrelated to a high degree within the model. The diagram below illustrates this interrelation.

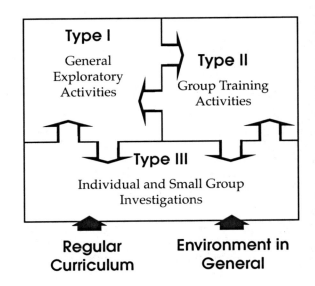

Overview for the Classroom Teacher

Classroom Management

The Enrichment Triad Model emphasizes high-quality outcomes for pupils that reflect the amount of understanding and the depth of thought of participating pupils. Depending upon ability in relation to the task at hand, pupils may start at any point within the model, however, allowing pupils to embark on Type III activities without background knowledge and training (Type I and II activities) may result in a poor or less than worthwhile investigation.

Type I

Pupils need to be given freedom to explore a variety of topics. This exploration must be purposeful and pupils must come up with some ideas for what they would like to study and how they will go about this.

For example: A pupil may be interested in insects. The pupil then looks at material related to insects and develops questions to be investigated. These may include:

- Why do insects have only six legs?
- Do all insects have the same body structure?
- What does an insect do?

The pupil will also come up with a plan to find the information to answer these questions. For example:

- An attendant at a local museum
- Finding and observing insects in their natural habitat

Teachers need to help pupils identify areas of study and stimulate interest. To start the process, ask pupils to talk about their interests. Once a pupil has identified an area of interest, the teacher needs to keep checking on progress by holding formal and informal meetings to discuss findings.

Type I activities should assist the teacher in deciding which Type II activities need to be taught to particular groups of pupils.

Type II

As these activities are training exercises to help the pupil deal more effectively with finding content, the teacher must ensure that the skills are first taught in a content-free lesson. Once the skills are internalized, the pupil can apply them to a specific task.

These skills focus on critical analysis, problem solving and divergent and creative thinking.

Type III

Not all pupils pursue an individual or small-group investigation for every topic. Type III enrichment activities are designed to:

◆ Foster a desire to find out more about a topic of interest.

◆ Provide an opportunity for those pupils who have shown interest, willingness and commitment to carry out an investigation of their own.

◆ Actively engage pupils in the formulation of a real issue and decision on a plan of action.

◆ Encourage pupils to produce new information for their topic and to present their findings to audiences for whom there is some relevance.

Renzulli's Enrichment Triad in Literacy

General

◆ Mastery of basic competencies in all areas needs to be made efficiently and rapidly through presentation that is exciting and relevant.

◆ Provide activities that are extra to the regular curriculum.

◆ Where necessary, provide opportunities for pupils to spend time with older groups to participate in curriculum-extension work.

◆ Arrange for pupils to work with mentors from within the school community or the local area.

◆ Take into account pupils' specific content interests and learning styles.

◆ Ensure that Type I activities involve little structure, but give some idea as to the type of investigation to be undertaken.

◆ Ensure that most enrichment activities are Type III activities.

Type I

◆ Set up interest centres related to themes or fields of study. These are to provoke curiosity rather than simply present information. For example:

- *Writing:* include advertising, literary criticism, journalism, poetry, play writing, short stories, autobiography etc.

- *Insects:* include fiction and non-fiction, start an ant farm, display dead insects.

◆ Invite an author to talk to the pupils about how they write their books.

◆ Conduct brainstorming activities where pupils list everything they wish to know about a topic.

◆ Organize an excursion to observe and gather information (for example, to a planetarium, museum, newspaper office, or radio station).

Type II

◆ Develop research skills – present the research cycle and carry out basic research projects. For example:

- Why do bees perform a dance on returning to the hive?

- What do authors include in a biography?

◆ Involve pupils in small-scale investigations requiring them to collect, record and communicate new information (for example compare the different types of advertising seen on TV during children's shows and between 6.30 and 7.30pm).

◆ Develop problem-solving strategies in your pupils. Ask questions that require problem identification, analysis and solution generation, at the same time developing an awareness of consequences of actions. For example:

- Imagine that telephone communications have been destroyed. How would we communicate quickly with other countries and areas?

Type III

◆ Ask pupils to formulate an issue and devise a plan of action to carry out the investigation.

◆ Provide ample time for individuals or small groups to carry out their investigation. Help them to develop a time schedule and build in regular progress checks.

◆ Encourage pupils to produce new information. For example:

- write a book

- develop a new product and its advertising campaign.

Name: _____

Type I – Advertising

Form small groups, with each choosing a different half-hour time slot to watch a TV channel that shows adverts, ie ITV, Channel 4. Note down which advertisements are run. (If possible, record them.)

From these adverts, complete the following:

1   Write down the products advertised.

Ad 1: _____   Ad 5: _____

Ad 2: _____   Ad 6: _____

Ad 3: _____   Ad 7: _____

Ad 4: _____   Ad 8: _____

2   Which advert did you like best and why?

_____

_____

3   Choose two adverts and write down what they said the product could do.

Product 1	Product 2
Name _____	Name _____

4   Identify the words used to persuade you to buy the product.

_____

_____

Write on a separate sheet:

5   From your findings as a group, are there any adverts that appear more than once? Which ones?

6   a)   Find an advert for one of these products in a magazine or newspaper. Compare this to the TV advert.

   b)   Write down the steps you would take when conducting an advertising campaign for a new product.

Name:

 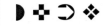
Type III – Investigation Plan

General Area of Study: _____

Specific Area of Study: _____

What will I need to do to get started?		List everything you'll need to start eg 'information I'll need to know', 'surveys I'll need to conduct' etc.
What resources will I need?		List reference material for information, any people you may need to talk to or get help from.
How will I go about my investigation?		List ways you'll gather your information - interviews, surveys, observations.
Who is my intended audience?		List the different types of people or groups interested in your findings or product.
How am I going to share my information?		List how you'll present your information.

Self-evaluation:

Things I did well:	Things I could do better:
Resources that were useful:	**Things that did not give me the information I needed:**

Type I → ● ◗ ♣

'Egyptology'

In a group of three, discuss which questions you would ask:

* the curator of a museum about Egyptian artefacts

* the Egyptian Embassy about Egypt.

Type II ❖ ⇒ ✖

Pyramid Capers

Describe the different types of buildings the Egyptian Pharaohs built.

List the methods used by the Pharaohs to build these.

Make a model of one of the pyramids.

Label the model including the Pharaoh who built it and why.

Type I ❖ ■ →

Investigating Egypt

From books on Egypt, pick a topic you would like to know more about.

Write down all the things you already know about your topic.

Write down at least six things you would like to find out about your topic.

Type II ⊃ ❖ ✶ ✖

Eco-Egypt

Many tourists visit the pyramids every year. The number of tourists walking on the pyramids, the erosion caused by the wind and the age of the structures are proving to be problems for the government of Egypt.

• Describe what the problems could be.

• Suggest how they could be overcome.

Renzulli's Enrichment Triad in Literacy
Theme: Insects

Type I

Bugs at Play

Find some insects in the playground.

Write down where you found them.

Observe these insects over three days and write down what you see the insects doing.

Type II

Insect Cartography

With two friends, walk around the playground looking for areas where insects live.

Write down what these areas look like. (Find at least three different areas.)

Draw a map of the school and mark the location of your insect habitats.

Compare your map and details with those of other members of the class.

Type I

Bug Fan Club

From books on insects, choose a creature you think is interesting.

Write five questions you would ask a 'bug expert' to gain more information about this insect.

List all the words you can think of that would describe this insect. Be as creative and thorough as you can.

Draw your insect surrounded by these words.

Type II

'Antz'

Watch the 'ANTZ' DVD.

List some of the problems faced by the ant colony in this movie and the solutions they came up with.

With a friend, come up with some alternative solutions to these problems.

Create a flow chart of your various solutions, including the consequences of each.

Renzulli's Enrichment Triad in Maths

General

◆ Ensure that pupils have a solid grasp of concepts by developmental instruction in all areas of mathematics.

◆ Design contracts and guidelines with realistic completion dates.

◆ Create skill centres that help pupils apply and extend particular skills (addition, subtraction, multiplication, division, problem solving) in real-life situations.

◆ Provide games that involve logic (for example: Cluedo, Monopoly, Chess and Mastermind).

Type I

◆ Provide task cards that ask pupils to brainstorm ideas for solving mathematical problems. For example: How many ways can you express the value shown by the numeral 5 in 756?

◆ Ask pupils to think of all the ways they use maths in everyday life.

◆ Give pupils mathematical terms and examples of their application in real-life situations.

◆ Invite a builder, carpenter, interior designer or architect to talk about the use of mathematics in their professions in relation to:

- Working out materials to be used and their cost

- Determining angles and pitches

- Drawing to scale and interpreting scale drawings.

Type II

◆ Assist pupils to develop skills in making and checking predictions by providing mathematical problems requiring them to think of questions for given answers. For example:

- Answer: There were only 14 pupils left on the bus.

- Answer: The travellers travelled 36km each day.

◆ Assist pupils to develop collecting, recording and communication skills by devising small-group research projects.

◆ Enhance pupils' research and reporting skills. For example: Provide pupils with the properties (size, colour, shape, dimensions etc.) of lesser-known objects. Ask them to name the objects, then sort them into different groups according to two similar attributes eg size and colour, usefulness and/or popularity etc.

◆ Ask pupils to identify and analyse problems and come up with various solutions.

Type III

◆ Assist pupils to work out their own plan for completion of their chosen topic before beginning their research project.

◆ Ask pupils to prepare and give a talk, predicting the outcome, prior to starting the project. On completion of the project, give another talk to confirm or refute their original predictions.

◆ Hold a `Maths Fair' where pupils present individual or small-group research projects to other year groups.

Name:

Type I – Everyday Maths

Every day we use many different types of mathematical operations.

1 Look at the activities on the trees below and write down all the ways you would use mathematics to complete them. We have done one for you. (Write your answers on a new sheet of paper.)

Buying three ice creams:

1. Find the cost of one ice cream. 2. Multiply that cost by three.
3. Check that you have enough money to pay for the ice creams.
4. Check you were given the correct change.

1. Determining who won the 800-metre race at the athletics carnival.

2. Winning a fishing competition with the biggest fish.

3. Deciding which CD to buy – a new release or two with 20% each discount.

4. Going to Cineworld for the day and seeing each film showing from the six screens.

5. Going to the cinema by bus.

6. Buying two takeaway meals.

7. Having new carpets put down throughout the house.

8. Buying a pair of jeans and a t-shirt.

2 With a friend, write down all the things you do during the day. Sort them into things that involve maths and things that don't.

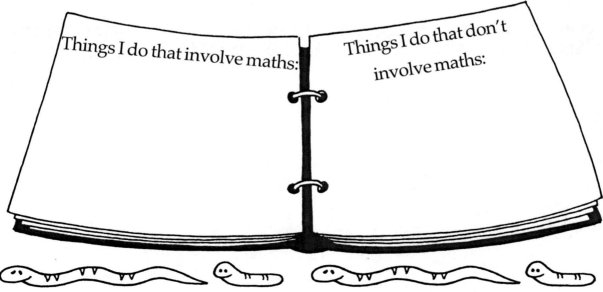

Things I do that involve maths:

Things I do that don't involve maths:

Name:

Management Strategies:

Type III – Investigating Maths

Topic of my investigation: _____

Before I begin my investigation:

Things I may need to do:	Things I may need to find out:

Things I hope to find out:	What I hope to do with my findings:

After completing my investigation:

Things I needed to do:	What I had to know:

What I found out:	What I will do with my findings:

Did your predictions match with what you really did and what you found out? _____

_____

_____

Renzulli's Enrichment Triad in Maths

Theme: Shopping

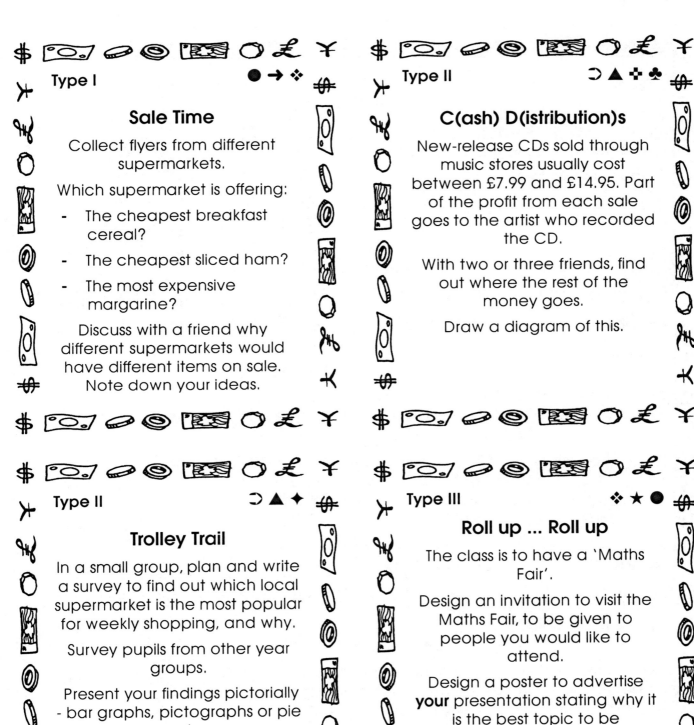

Type I

Sale Time

Collect flyers from different supermarkets.

Which supermarket is offering:

- The cheapest breakfast cereal?

- The cheapest sliced ham?

- The most expensive margarine?

Discuss with a friend why different supermarkets would have different items on sale. Note down your ideas.

Type II

C(ash) D(istribution)s

New-release CDs sold through music stores usually cost between £7.99 and £14.95. Part of the profit from each sale goes to the artist who recorded the CD.

With two or three friends, find out where the rest of the money goes.

Draw a diagram of this.

Type II

Trolley Trail

In a small group, plan and write a survey to find out which local supermarket is the most popular for weekly shopping, and why.

Survey pupils from other year groups.

Present your findings pictorially - bar graphs, pictographs or pie graphs.

Make some statements about the shopping habits of your survey group.

Type III

Roll up ... Roll up

The class is to have a 'Maths Fair'.

Design an invitation to visit the Maths Fair, to be given to people you would like to attend.

Design a poster to advertise **your** presentation stating why it is the best topic to be presented at the Fair.

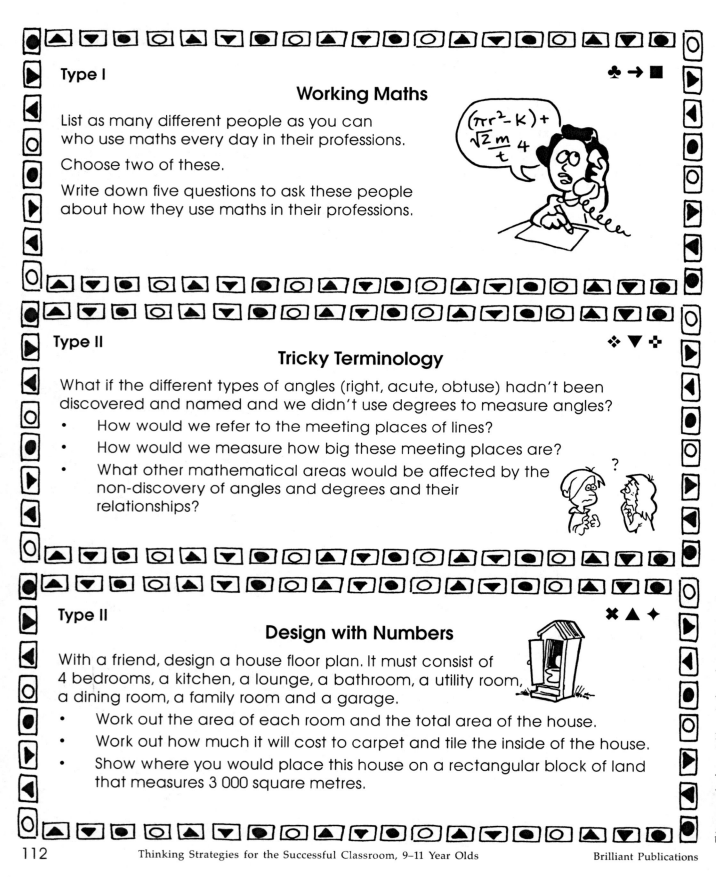

Type I

Working Maths

♣ → ■

List as many different people as you can who use maths every day in their professions.

Choose two of these.

Write down five questions to ask these people about how they use maths in their professions.

Type II

Tricky Terminology

❖ ▼ ✤

What if the different types of angles (right, acute, obtuse) hadn't been discovered and named and we didn't use degrees to measure angles?

- How would we refer to the meeting places of lines?
- How would we measure how big these meeting places are?
- What other mathematical areas would be affected by the non-discovery of angles and degrees and their relationships?

Type II

Design with Numbers

✖ ▲ ✦

With a friend, design a house floor plan. It must consist of 4 bedrooms, a kitchen, a lounge, a bathroom, a utility room, a dining room, a family room and a garage.

- Work out the area of each room and the total area of the house.
- Work out how much it will cost to carpet and tile the inside of the house.
- Show where you would place this house on a rectangular block of land that measures 3 000 square metres.

Renzulli's Enrichment Triad in Science

General

◆ Create learning centres related to themes across curriculum areas or devoted to different areas of science: meteorology, ecology, pollution, astrology, genetics, electronics, biology, famous scientists etc.

◆ Ensure that pupils have mastered terms and concepts related to science by exposing them to a curriculum that is developmental.

◆ Help pupils to learn to solve problems creatively – there is not always a right or a wrong answer.

◆ Encourage pupils to question what they see: 'How did that happen?'

◆ Encourage curiosity with displays showing an end result rather than the beginning only (for example, different paper aeroplanes that fly well, and cards that ask for pupils' opinions as to why they fly so well).

Type I

◆ To arouse curiosity about how science works, provide simple experiments for pupils to perform.

◆ To create interest, display newspaper and magazine articles about different topics related to themes or science disciplines. For example:

- Inventions related to air travel.

- Life cycle of living things such as toads and frogs, butterflies, dragonflies etc.

◆ Organize a trip to the local science centre.

◆ Invite guest speakers to talk about their area of interest.

Type II

◆ Encourage the development of divergent questioning skills by using open-ended questions. For example:

- What are the ways in which birds find food?

- How is a moth's life cycle similar to and different from that of a human being?

◆ Ask pupils to collect, record and communicate their findings when solving crimes using different forensic science techniques.

◆ Organize for pupils to walk around the playground/local area (supervised) to observe and write down the different animals, birds and insects, noting the number and location of the creatures. Pupils can then present these observations to the class either orally, in writing or as diagrams.

◆ Ask pupils to complete research topics to help them identify methods, questioning techniques and information- gathering strategies.

Type III

◆ Ask pupils to identify why they wish to follow through with their investigation and why it is being done individually or in a small group.

◆ Ask pupils to identify their audience and present their findings appropriately.

◆ Engage mentors, peer tutors, parents and other teachers to help pupils carry out and complete their investigations.

Name: _____

Type I – Inventions

1 From books on inventions, choose one that you would like to investigate.

The invention I will investigate is: _____

2 Write down five things that you already know about this invention.

3 Write down four things that you would like to know about this invention.

1 _____   3 _____

2 _____   4 _____

4 Change one component in this invention. What effect would this have?

The component I changed:	What the new component looks like:
_____	_____
_____	_____
_____	_____
How it will work now?	**Did I improve the invention?**
_____	
_____	
_____	

Name:

Type II – Forensic Science

With your forensic science team – photographer, fingerprint expert, questioner (who decides who to question and what to ask), microscope analyst (who decides what to take as evidence) – describe the steps you would take to solve the following crime:

The librarian has been shot and killed in the library after the annual Book Fair. The library office has been ransacked and it looks like there has been a struggle. There is a note saying: 'Thank you for the holiday money. It is greatly appreciated.' A large sum of money is missing. Three staff members (the deputy head, the PE teacher and the year 1 head teacher) were seen leaving the school grounds late on the day of the murder.

1 Write down what each expert would do in the order they would do it:

Photographer	Fingerprint Expert
1 _____	1 _____
2 _____	2 _____
3 _____	3 _____
4 _____	4 _____

Questioner	Microscope Analyst
1 _____	1 _____
2 _____	2 _____
3 _____	3 _____
4 _____	4 _____

(Use a separate sheet of paper.)

2 How does your team think the murder took place?

3 How will your team prove your suspicions?

4 Write down how you will present your findings to the court so that your suspect will be convicted of this crime.

Renzulli's Enrichment Triad in Humanities

General

◆ This area of the curriculum should be linked with as many other areas as possible.

◆ Within humanities, areas that can be explored include genealogy, demography, philosophy, anthropology, consumerism etc.

◆ Create learning/interest centres (see page 8) that explore universal themes and values such as family, friendship, conformity, initiative and vision, peace and independence etc.

◆ Assist pupils to identify different aspects of communication: point of view, evaluative judgements, arguments, subjectivity and objectivity, empathy, prejudice etc.

Type I

◆ Ask pupils to identify areas they would like to study. Group pupils according to their interests and ask them to identify particular areas to investigate.

◆ Organize a debate about issues to do with the community, present government and school rules. Group these into broad areas and develop a web of related issues that pupils may wish to pursue.

◆ Present film footage about how communities get along. Ask pupils to identify issues and solutions portrayed in the clip.

◆ Provide pupils with task cards from identified areas of interest.

◆ Visit the local or county council to observe how decisions are made and how these forums are conducted.

Type II

◆ Engage pupils in discussions that involve moral and ethical issues.

◆ Ask pupils to prepare and complete questionnaires, surveys and interviews that require them to search for and state subjects' values, attitudes and beliefs on topics. For example:

- People with blue eyes are superior to people who have green or brown eyes.

- People who have a disability are not as clever as those who do not have a disability.

◆ Organize pupil role-plays related to government decision making. Pupils take on roles of specific members of parliament and debate a topic from that member's point of view.

◆ Ask pupils to find out the demography of the local community and identify the different groups represented. Identify the needs of the community and write letters to local government bodies in relation to these.

Type III

◆ Involve pupils in an individual or small-group investigation of their own choosing.

◆ Assist pupils to plan their investigation, listing how they intend to conduct it and the help they may need along the way.

◆ Ask pupils to present the findings of their investigation to the rest of the class or to other interested parties. Encourage them to use a variety of media and presentation forms.

Name:

Type I, II – Local Government

Answer the following questions before you visit the Council Chambers:

What do you expect to see at the Council meeting?	
What do you think the Councillors will be discussing?	
What do you think the job of the Mayor involves?	
Write three questions you would like to ask during question time:	

Answer these questions after your visit:

Who was at the meeting?	
What was discussed?	
What does the Mayor do?	
Were you satisfied with the answers to your questions?	

Having visited Council Chambers, what aspect of local government would you like to investigate?

_____

_____

_____

Renzulli's Enrichment Triad in Creative Arts

General

◆ Pupils should be able to experience all aspects of this curriculum during free time as well as during specific learning experiences.

◆ Ensure that pupils experience all aspects of creative thinking such as fluency, flexibility, originality, elaboration, curiosity, complexity, risk-taking and imagination.

◆ Include in this area of study: periods of art; contemporary artists; art and its contribution to society; design related to clothes, toys, furniture and buildings; calligraphy; animated film making; graphics; and puppetry.

◆ Display around the room works of art by great masters, pupils and local artists.

Type I

◆ Invite local artists to talk about how they produce their work.

◆ Arrange for local artists to conduct workshops in a variety of media.

◆ Visit an art gallery or view slides of works by masters and discuss these in different terms (for example: like/dislike; texture; form; colour; tone; and line).

◆ Provide different media for pupils to work with and allow them to experiment with techniques.

Type II

◆ Organize debates about the techniques of 20th century artists such as Andy Warhol.

◆ Ask pupils to research the life and work of an artist. On completion, group pupils according to the style of the various artists chosen. Ask them to discuss similarities or differences in their works.

◆ Show pupils pictures of different styles of house (Elizabethan, Victorian, modern etc) and ask them to discuss the design features within each of the different eras of architecture.

◆ Discuss with pupils how art has reflected society over the ages.

◆ Ask pupils to design an item of clothing that could have been worn during Elizabethan times or during the 1960s.

◆ Ask pupils to critique their own art for a school magazine.

Type III

◆ Pupils produce a piece of artwork using a technique of their own.

◆ Assist pupils to produce a plan of their artwork including initial sketches and preliminary thoughts on how the piece will look.

◆ Assist pupils to plan a time frame for the completion of their artwork.

◆ Hold an exhibition of student artwork for the school and local community.

Name:

Management Strategies:

RENZULLI'S TRIAD

Creative Arts

Worksheet 44

Type II – Puppetry

Design three puppets that demonstrate the effects of habitat destruction. They must not be made from anything that would lead to habitat destruction.

1   In the spaces below, write down your rough ideas for the three puppets.

Puppet 1	Puppet 2	Puppet 3

2   On a separate sheet of paper, plan what your puppet will look like and how you will make it.

3   Explain each puppet's connection to habitat destruction and how it will help get the message about the effects of this across to others.

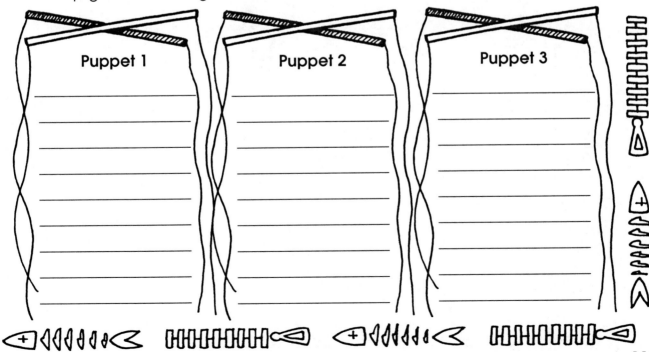

Gardner's Multiple Intelligences

by **Fay Holbert**
and **Margaret Bishop**

Overview for the Classroom Teacher

Introduction to Howard Gardner's 'Multiple Intelligences'

Gardner defines intelligence as 'the ability to solve problems, or to create products, that are valued within one or more cultural setting/s'. He maintains that it should be possible to identify an individual's educational profile at an early age, and then draw upon this knowledge to enhance that person's educational opportunities and options. An educator should be able to channel individuals with unusual talents into special enrichment schemes. To this end, he has developed a framework, building on the theory of multiple intelligences, that can be applied to any educational situation.

Because of Gardner's work, many educators believe that education is not merely a means to sort out a few children and make them leaders, but to develop the latent talents of the entire population in diverse ways.

If we are to understand our children's potential, we must take into consideration all of their abilities and not just those that can be tested with standardized instruments such as an IQ test. What is important in educational terms is not which intelligences we are strongest in, but our own particular blend of strengths and weaknesses.

The importance attached to the IQ however is not entirely inappropriate – the score does predict a person's ability to achieve in school subjects. Its limitation is that it predicts little of the successes in later life.

So, what of the wider range of performances that are valued in different parts of the world? For example: a 12-year-old boy from the Caroline Islands who has shown some ability is selected by his elders to learn how to become a master sailor and undertake study of navigation, geography and the stars; and a 15-year-old Iranian youth who has committed to heart the entire Koran and mastered the Arabic language will train to be a teacher and religious leader.

It is obvious that these two young people are displaying intelligent behaviour, and it is equally clear that the present method of assessing intellect is not going to allow an accurate assessment of their potential or their achievements. Only if we expand and rethink our views of what counts as human intellect will we, as educators, be able to devise more appropriate ways of assessing it, and more effective ways of educating it.

Gardner's 'Intelligences' are:

- Verbal/Linguistic
- Logical/Mathematical
- Visual/Spatial
- Bodily/Kinaesthetic
- Musical/Rhythmical
- Interpersonal
- Intrapersonal

Recently Gardner has added a new intelligence: Nature/Environmental.

Learning/Interest Centres

The classroom teacher should give equal time and attention to each intelligence every day. One way to achieve this is to maintain various learning/interest centres in the classroom. For example:

- The William Shakespeare Centre **(Verbal/Linguistic)**
- The Albert Einstein Centre **(Logical/Mathematical)**
- The Leonardo da Vinci Centre **(Visual/Spatial)**
- The Roger Bannister Movement **(Bodily/Kinaesthetic)**
- The Mozart Centre **(Musical/Rhythmical)**
- The Mary Seacole Centre **(Interpersonal)**
- The Helen Keller Centre **(Intrapersonal)**
- The David Attenborough Centre **(Nature/Environmental)**

A Note About This Section

This section looks at one theme from the perspective of the various 'intelligences'.

Overview for the Classroom Teacher

Details and Description of Gardner's 'Multiple Intelligences'

Verbal/Linguistic (V/L)

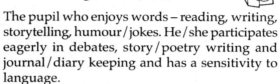

The pupil who enjoys words – reading, writing, storytelling, humour/jokes. He/she participates eagerly in debates, story/poetry writing and journal/diary keeping and has a sensitivity to language.

Writer, poet, novelist, journalist, psycho-linguist (L/M), signing.

Logical/Mathematical (L/M)

The pupil who loves numbers, patterns, relationships, formulae. He/she shines at mathematics, reasoning, logic, problem solving, deciphering codes and enjoys pattern games, calculation, number sequences, outlining.

Scientist, mathematician, engineer, technician.

Visual/Spatial (V/S)

The pupil who loves drawing, building, designing, creating, visualizing colours, pictures, observing, patterns/designs. He/she enjoys creating models, mind-mapping, pretending and has an active imagination.

Artist, cartographer, navigator, decorator, chess player.

Bodily/Kinaesthetic (B/K)

The pupil who has to touch, move, handle objects. He/she enjoys dance, drama, role-play, mime, sports games, physical gestures, martial arts and is great with body control, refining movement, expression through movement, inventing, interaction.

Athlete, surgeon (L/M), dancer/ choreographer (M/R).

Musical/Rhythmical (M/R)

The pupil who loves sounds, melody, rhythm, playing instruments, singing, vocal sounds/ tones. He/she needs to be involved with music composition/creation, music performances and enjoys percussion, humming, environmental/ instrumental sounds, tonal and rhythmic patterns.

Musician, composer, sound engineer (L/M), music critic (V/L).

Interpersonal (Ier)

The pupil who likes interacting, talking, giving and receiving feedback, group projects, cooperative learning strategies, division of labour. He/she needs to be involved in collaborative tasks and person-to-person communication. This pupil is always intuitive to others' feelings and motives and is empathetic.

Administrator, coach, mental health, physician (L/M), teacher (various).

Intrapersonal (Ira)

The pupil who wants to work alone, pursue personal interests, understands self, has introspective feelings and dreams. He/she displays silent reflective methods, higher-order reasoning and metacognition techniques, emotional processing, focus/concentration skills, complex guided imagery and 'centring' practices.

Writer (V/L), inventor (L/M).

Nature/Environmental (N/E)

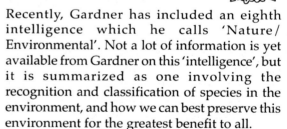

Recently, Gardner has included an eighth intelligence which he calls 'Nature/ Environmental'. Not a lot of information is yet available from Gardner on this 'intelligence', but it is summarized as one involving the recognition and classification of species in the environment, and how we can best preserve this environment for the greatest benefit to all.

Veterinarian, zoologist, botanist, national park ranger, landscape gardener (V/L), florist.

Note: the 'pupils' illustrated here appear on the task cards and worksheets that follow to indicate the 'intelligence' to which that activity is primarily targeted.

Gardner's Multiple Intelligences, Activities

Theme: Ancient Civilizations – What They Gave Us

Many of the activities that follow are not exclusive to one intelligence, but may involve two or more. For example, those asking for illustrations involve Visual/Spatial and those requiring oral and/or written presentations involve Verbal/Linguistic.

Where questions could be answered with a 'yes' or 'no' response, probe for more information.

The activities that follow concentrate mainly on civilizations BC.

Verbal/Linguistic

- What is the meaning of 'civilization'?
- What is the meaning of 'ancient'?
- What is meant by 'hunters and gatherers'? How and why did this type of existence change?
- How many words can you find in your dictionary that derive from the Latin 'civis'?
- Prior to writing, how were stories, facts and history kept and passed on?

Logical/Mathematical

- The Great Pyramid has a base that would hold six football fields. How does the school playground compare?
- The Great Pyramid is 40 storeys high – approximately 138 metres. How many times taller than your school is that?
- Why would these people keep a 'tally'?
- Why was it important to know the length of a year and of daylight?
- How large were cities 2 500 years ago? Were they bigger than your town/city?
- What did farmers do with crops or animals they couldn't use?
- How were workers and slaves paid?
- How did farmers water their crops?

Visual/Spatial

- How often does your family read maps? What is your most commonly used map?
- On a map of the world, where were Sumer, Egypt, Mesopotamia, Crete, Greece, China, Persia and the Indus Valley? Are they still known by these names?
- Why were so many temples and palaces built?
- What do wall and cave paintings tell us?

Bodily/Kinaesthetic

- What types of building skills were needed in ancient civilizations?
- What types of handicraft were valued?
- What would children have played with?
- How might the men have kept fit for war?

Musical/Rhythmical

- Why were music and dance so important?
- What sort of musical/rhythmical instruments might have been used?
- Other than dance, why might a steady rhythm or clear sound have been important?
- What could have been used for making instruments?

Interpersonal

- What types of occupations existed?
- Who made laws in these towns and cities?
- How were they different from our laws?
- How did people travel?
- Were there equal rights for men and women? How do we know?

Intrapersonal

- Which civilization would you like to have been a member of? Which one would you not like to join? Why?
- Which occupation would you have chosen?
- Which invention/creation/development was the most important for mankind?

Nature/Environmental

- Why was the farmers' soil rich?
- What is irrigation?
- What types of crops were grown?
- Which animals were kept?
- Why did people eat meat at celebrations?
- How were plants and animals used, other than for food?

Activities for Ancient Civilizations

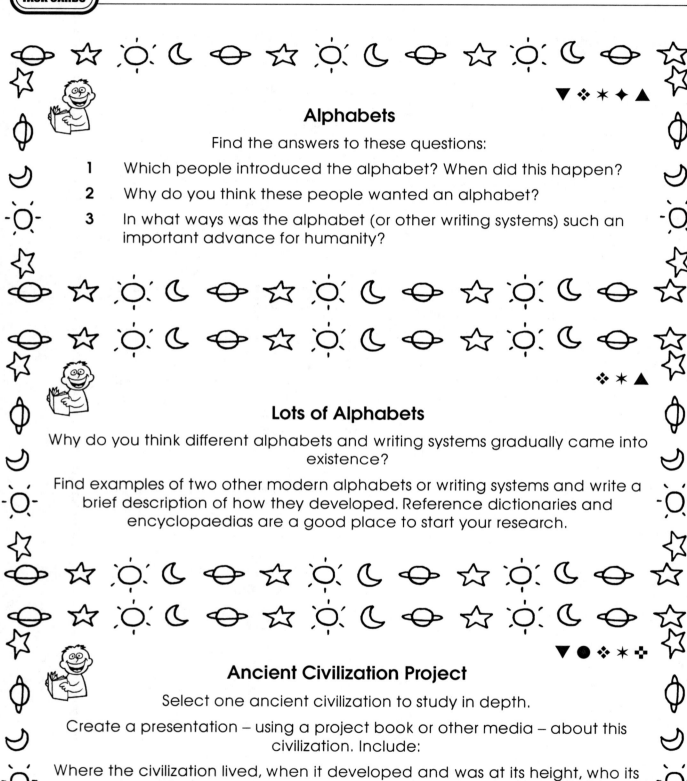

Alphabets

Find the answers to these questions:

1 Which people introduced the alphabet? When did this happen?

2 Why do you think these people wanted an alphabet?

3 In what ways was the alphabet (or other writing systems) such an important advance for humanity?

Lots of Alphabets

Why do you think different alphabets and writing systems gradually came into existence?

Find examples of two other modern alphabets or writing systems and write a brief description of how they developed. Reference dictionaries and encyclopaedias are a good place to start your research.

Ancient Civilization Project

Select one ancient civilization to study in depth.

Create a presentation – using a project book or other media – about this civilization. Include:

Where the civilization lived, when it developed and was at its height, who its leaders were, what kinds of technology were developed, information about its culture, major achievements, reason/s for its rise and fall.

Activities for Ancient Civilizations

▼ ❖ ✖ ✦ ◆

Weights and Measures

As trade was one of the main reasons for
the success or failure of a civilization, weights and measures
were vital to both sellers and buyers.

One such weight measure was a 'grain balance'. Draw a diagram of this.

With a partner, construct a working model of the balance so you can
demonstrate to the class how it worked.

▼ ❖ ✖ ◆

The Importance of Ports

Why was it important for ancient civilizations to be near a river
and/or the sea?

On a map of the world, show where these civilizations were found:

Sumer, Phoenicia, Egypt, Babylon, Mycenae, Crete, Persia.

Are they still known by the same name?

Note their location in relation to water.

→ ■ ◗ ✶ ◻

Ancient Arts and Crafts

Search through reference books, encyclopaedias and magazines to find
pictures or photographs of the jewellery worn by the people of these ancient
communities. Also find illustrations of the pottery created.

Either, using beads, modelling clay and nylon thread (and the illustrations you
have found), create some replica jewellery of these times,

or, paint and decorate an earthenware pot in the style of an ancient artisan.

Name:

Comparative Sizes

1   Compare the size and capacity of these buildings:

Structure	Area of Base	Spectator Capacity
The Colosseum		
Wembley Stadium		
Sydney Opera House		

2   Compare the dimensions of these buildings:

Structure	Length	Width	Height
The Great Pyramid of Giza			
The Post Office Tower			
Houses of Parliament			

3   What are the main differences between the ancient and the modern buildings in terms of how they have been built?

Write your thoughts here:

Did you know that the base of the Great Pyramid, completed in 2528 BC, is a perfect square to within 15mm? During a period of about 20 years, 200 000 slaves moved 2 500 000 stones for its construction.

Name:

Town Planning

About 2500 BC, the people of the Indus Valley had town planners who planned the houses in city blocks, separated by roads nine metres wide. They even drew up city maps!

1   Draw a map of your community showing where you live, play and learn.

2   What is the population of your town/city/village? _____

3   Over 3500 years ago, the population of Babylon was approximately 200 000. Name six cities and/or towns today that have a population of approximately the same as ancient Babylon.

1 _____   2 _____

3 _____   4 _____

5 _____   6 _____

4   What is the population of the UK, according to the last census?

_____

Did you know that a census taken about 2 000 years ago in China showed that the Han-ruled states had a total population of 59 594 978?

Name:

Measuring Time

Early civilizations had instruments for measuring time, but they were not very reliable.

1 Explain how these instruments operated and illustrate each one.

Sundial	Candle Clock
Water Clock	Hourglass

2 Now complete the table below:

Timepiece	Where?	When?	Disadvantages
Sundial			
Water Clock			
Candle Clock			
Hourglass			

Thinking Strategies for the Successful Classroom, 9–11 Year Olds

Brilliant Publications

Name:

Management Strategies:
▼ ❖ ■
◗ ★ ✚ ▲

GARDNER'S MULTIPLE INTELLIGENCES
Worksheet 48

Ancient Irrigation Systems

The growing cities of Babylon, Çatalhöyük, Memphis and Mohenjo-Daro now had tradesmen, artisans and officials who traded their services for the food they needed. As a result, the farmers had to increase their food production. To do this, they needed larger farms and a way to water their crops. They began to irrigate their land. They used a shaduf and later a treadmill.

1   Illustrate these two devices.

Shaduf	Treadmill

2   How did each help to irrigate the land?

Shaduf

Treadmill

3   With a partner, make a model of a waterwheel and demonstrate to the class how it functioned.

Activities for Ancient Civilizations

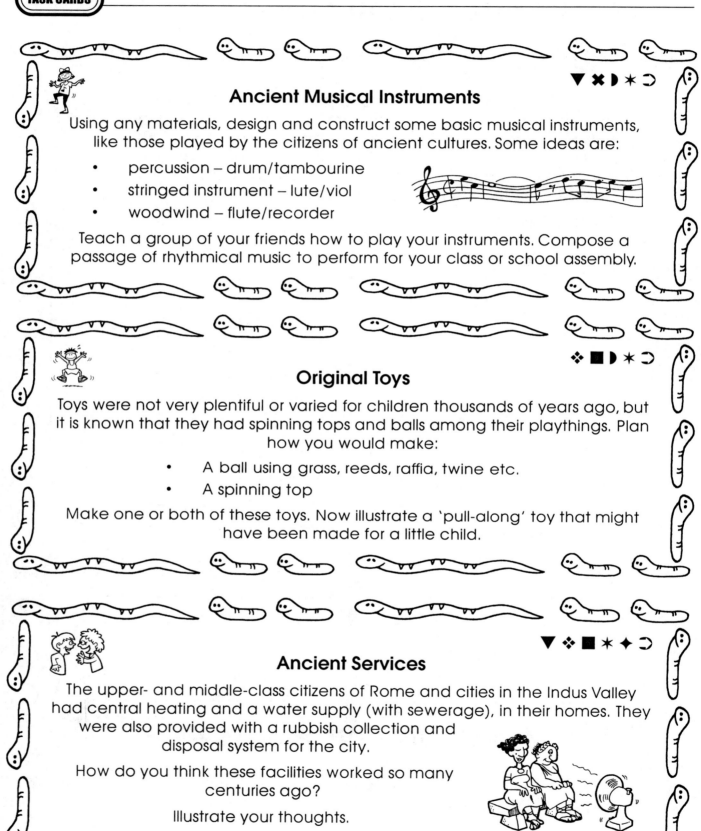

Ancient Musical Instruments

▼ ✖ ◗ ✳ ⊃

Using any materials, design and construct some basic musical instruments, like those played by the citizens of ancient cultures. Some ideas are:

- percussion – drum/tambourine
- stringed instrument – lute/viol
- woodwind – flute/recorder

Teach a group of your friends how to play your instruments. Compose a passage of rhythmical music to perform for your class or school assembly.

Original Toys

❖ ◼◗ ✳ ⊃

Toys were not very plentiful or varied for children thousands of years ago, but it is known that they had spinning tops and balls among their playthings. Plan how you would make:

- A ball using grass, reeds, raffia, twine etc.
- A spinning top

Make one or both of these toys. Now illustrate a 'pull-along' toy that might have been made for a little child.

Ancient Services

▼ ❖ ◼ ✳ ◆ ⊃

The upper- and middle-class citizens of Rome and cities in the Indus Valley had central heating and a water supply (with sewerage), in their homes. They were also provided with a rubbish collection and disposal system for the city.

How do you think these facilities worked so many centuries ago?

Illustrate your thoughts.

Activities for Ancient Civilizations

The Importance of Music

Why was music and dance such an important part of the lives of the people who lived hundreds and thousands of years ago?

Complete this chart, giving some reasons:

Wealthy/Upper Class	Middle Class	Poorer Class/Slaves
1.		
2.		
3.		
4.		
5.		

Soldiers' Health Regimen

Plan a daily health and physical fitness programme for soldiers in the army of Sparta.

In some nations, all men were required to be ready to go to war whenever their ruler decided to fight another nation.

Time	Food	Arms/Shoulders	Body	Legs

Activities for Ancient Civilizations

Olympic Games

In the Olympic Games, and other adult athletic competitions, what is the Marathon?

Why is this event given this name?

Who ran the very first Marathon?

The Importance of Coins

Business had been carried on using a trading or bartering system for many thousands of years. Coinage was introduced in Persia about 500 BC and in China about 220 BC.

How would this have changed the daily activities of the traders and other business people?

Ancient Entertainment

How were the people entertained in ancient Babylon, Egypt, Athens and/or Rome?

Illustrate some of their pastimes and amusements.

Name:

Government

Over 2 500 years ago, the Greeks overthrew the 'aristocracy' and installed a 'democracy'.

1   What do these two words mean?

Aristocracy

Democracy

2   Illustrate how a democracy works:

In what ways was the Greek democracy different from ours?

3   Organize a democratic election for a 'Study Centres Monitor' for your class.

Name:

Ancient Medicine

Would you like to have been a doctor in Egypt or the Indus Valley 2 000 years ago?

The first-known textbook on surgery was written by the Egyptians about 2500 BC.

The first hospital and rest homes were built in the Indus Valley by King Asoka about 300 BC.

If a doctor failed to heal a rich patient he was severely punished, sometimes even killed. If he failed to heal a slave his punishment was only a payment to the master.

1 Who was Hippocrates and how do we remember him today?

_____

2 Who are some famous, modern-day physicians and surgeons and what have they accomplished for society?

	Doctor	When?	What?
1.			
2.			
3.			
4.			
5.			
6.			
7.			

Brilliant Publications

Activities for Ancient Civilizations

Jobs for the Boys

As boys grew up in ancient times, they had a wide range of occupations to choose from – if they were not slaves.

Name some of the jobs that were open to boys in these areas:

- handicraft
- sciences
- arts
- building
- designing

Lives of Girls

As girls grew up, what did they plan for the future?

Make a list of all your ideas.

Food: Then and Now

Research the types of food eaten in these ancient cultures.

What types of crops did farmers produce?

Make a list of all the kinds of food.

Now compare this to the food we eat today.

List those that are no longer eaten.

Ancient Animals

Name the animals that were used for the purposes listed below:

1. as food
2. for work
3. in war
4. as pets
5. in religious matters

Activities for Ancient Civilizations

Hammurabi's Codes

Hammurabi, King of Mesopotamia in about 1792 BC, brought great changes to the laws of his country. Two of his laws were:

1.   Wrongdoers were judged and punished by the decision of society, rather than by the victim and/or the victim's family.

2.   All killings were treated as murder.

List the **advantages** and the **disadvantages** of these two laws.

Features of Ancient Civilizations

What can you find out about these features of ancient civilizations?

Quipu_____

_____

Ziggurat_____

_____

Petroglyphs_____

_____

Obsidian_____

_____

Shaduf _____

_____

Rosetta Stone_____

_____

Name:

Management
Strategies:

GARDNER'S
MULTIPLE
INTELLIGENCES
Worksheet 51

The Wheel

The wheel was first invented in Sumer about 3500 BC. By about 3250 BC the first wheeled vehicles were used there.

1   How do you think the idea of the wheel might first have come to the Sumerians? Write your thoughts here:

2   How might the first wheels have been made? _____

_____

3   List the improvements made by the wheel for these people.

Rulers	Traders	Farmers	Others

4   Which people might have benefited most from the wheel?

Illustrate your reasons here.

Gardner's Multiple Intelligences, Activities

Theme: The Future – What Will Life Be Like?

Many of the suggested activities engage more than one of the intelligences. Students should be encouraged to attempt a wide range of activities and be aware of the various intelligences they are using.

Verbal/Linguistic

◆ Make Word Bank Posters of any words that you think will change their meaning in the future or any new words that will be invented.

◆ Write a news report, poem or story about what your life will be like in the future.

◆ What different types of jobs will people have in the future? Will there be new job titles and descriptions?

◆ Will people still write and read stories? Think of other ways to share stories.

◆ How will people communicate in the future?

Logical/Mathematical

◆ Construct a time-line showing milestones in your own future, eg your 18th birthday, finishing your education, getting married, starting a family!

◆ Ask your classmates what they think they will be doing 50 years from now, eg work, family, travel etc. Record your findings on a bar chart or a pie chart.

◆ Space travel may be commonplace in the future. Investigate the distances between the Earth and planets we may visit or even live on.

◆ Estimate the time it would take to travel to each of the planets in our solar system.

◆ Buildings may be very different in shape and size in the future. Talk about the designs for future housing/buildings to meet energy needs, and any other designs needed to stop changes happening to the environment (eg cars and their emissions).

◆ Will time still be measured in 24-hour periods and the units of day, week, month and year still be relevant? What might replace this basis for time measurement?

Visual/Spatial

◆ Design an advertisement to promote a future settlement on Mars (or any other potentially habitable planet).

◆ Design clothing that would be worn in the future. What fabrics will be used? Will there be any special safety considerations?

◆ Create a map that will help people find their way around your neighbourhood in the future. Think about what will have changed, new buildings, different road systems and so on.

◆ How will the future look (especially 200 years from now)? What will have changed? (You could ask older relatives or friends to tell you about the changes they've seen since they were young children.)

Bodily/Kinaesthetic

◆ What new skills will be needed in the future (for example, manufacturing, agriculture and technology)?

◆ Will people still move in the same way or will changes to the Earth's environment affect our ability to walk, run or jump?

◆ Take turns in a small group miming everyday activities that people will perform in the future. Consider what activities may be different in the future.

◆ Brainstorm ideas for keeping healthy and fit in the future.

◆ Write and perform a play set in the distant future. Will people still communicate the same way?

◆ What sport will be played in the future?

◆ Create a new dance that will become all the rage in the future.

Gardner's Multiple Intelligences, Activities

Musical/Rhythmical

◆ Will music and dance still have an important role in the future?

◆ Record some music that you think will be popular with teenagers in the future.

◆ What new instruments will be invented? Will people still play the instruments that are used today?

◆ Will music be used in advertising, eg jingles, raps?

◆ If aliens are found to be living on other planets, do you think that music will be a part of their culture?

◆ Create a new style of music for the future and give it a catchy name.

Interpersonal

◆ Tell a partner three things that you plan to do before you are 75 years old.

◆ Will people still work in groups, eg staff at factories, schools, hospitals and offices? What changes do you foresee?

◆ Play 'Future Celebrity Heads' based on people who will be famous in the future.

◆ In groups of three or four, investigate one particular aspect of the future and share your findings with the whole class.

◆ Will the laws of today still be in existence? Will there have to be new laws for new circumstances?

◆ Will there be any new or different social problems in the future?

Intrapersonal

◆ Write a journal or diary entry for one day in your life if you were alive in 3020.

◆ Write a job application listing the personal attributes (including your strengths and weaknesses) that would make you a suitable candidate for a job 200 years from now.

◆ You are going to run for leader of a new settlement on Mars. Decide on your campaign slogan and the platform you will run on (policies).

◆ If you could change one thing about today's world to make a better future, what would it be? Why do you want this change?

◆ What is your favourite film or book that is set in the future? Why do you like it? Ask your friends the same questions.

◆ You have been asked to lead an expedition into unknown territory on a newly settled planet.
Describe your feelings about the task ahead.

Nature/Environmental

◆ What will the natural environment be like in the future? Will there be climate change as a result of greenhouse gases and other problems of today?

◆ Will farms still provide our fresh food and food for processing? Will there be new ways of producing food?

◆ Many people today enjoy outdoor activities. Will this still be a feature of family leisure time in the future?

◆ There are many endangered species in the world today. What will be the situation in the future?

◆ Current space exploration is expanding our knowledge of other planets in our solar system. If we were to find plants and animals (flora and fauna) on any of these planets, what would they be like?

Activities for the Future

What's the News?

How will the news be reported in the future?

You are a reporter in the year 2095. Write an article about an event that has taken place. Don't forget to write a great headline!

Design a news information system that will be used in the future and 'publish' your article.

Future News

There are often reports in newspapers, magazines and on television suggesting what the world might be like in the future. Collect articles and sort them into the various topics they discuss, eg transport, food, housing and so on.

Start a class scrapbook of all the articles you've collected. Leave pages blank so new articles can be added to each topic.

The class scrapbook will be a great research tool.

Looking into the Future

Create a 'Focus on the Future Wall' in your classroom.

Collect posters, photos and drawings of what things may look like in the future and write a caption for each picture.

Mount the pictures and captions on sheets of card and then display them on the classroom wall.

Take turns being a 'Futures Guide' and conduct tours of the 'Focus on the Future Wall'.

Activities for the Future – Communities

GARDNER'S MULTIPLE INTELLIGENCES TASK CARDS

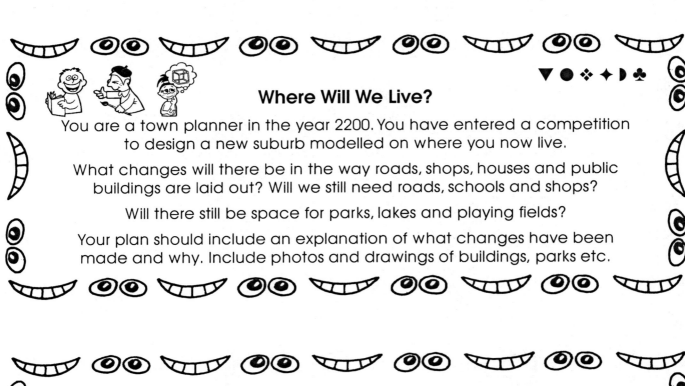

Where Will We Live?

▼ ● ❖ ◆ ❱ ♣

You are a town planner in the year 2200. You have entered a competition to design a new suburb modelled on where you now live.

What changes will there be in the way roads, shops, houses and public buildings are laid out? Will we still need roads, schools and shops?

Will there still be space for parks, lakes and playing fields?

Your plan should include an explanation of what changes have been made and why. Include photos and drawings of buildings, parks etc.

What Will School Be Like?

▼ ❖ ❱ ✳ ▲

Form a 'Futures Planning Committee' with three or four of your classmates. Your task, as students at a school of today, is to prepare and present a report about the schools of the future that your grandchildren may attend.

Your report should consider the following questions:

What subjects will be studied? Include a list of the topics that might be part of the school curriculum in the future.

What about teachers? How will the curriculum be taught?

Will schools still have buildings and playgrounds and be located in communities as they are now?

In the future, will you still have to go to school 6 hours a day, 5 days a week? What might be different?

What resources will there be to help you learn? Libraries? Computers? Books?

FUTURE CHALLENGE: Design a School of the Future

Name:

Earth in the Future – Changing Names – Changing Places

1 What's That Country?

Throughout history, many countries have changed names or borders. On the map below, mark any changes in borders or country names that you think may occur in the future. Explain why you think these changes may take place.

2 Earth Watch

Will there be any changes to the physical shape of the landmasses owing to climatic or other events? As a scientist in the year 2104, you are trying to deal with problems caused in the past. Write a report to send back in time, warning the people on Earth what the results have been of not controlling the problems of the 21st century and earlier.

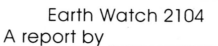

Earth Watch 2104

A report by _____

This page may be photocopied for use by the purchasing institution only.
© Blake Education Pty Ltd. 2004

Management Strategies:

▼ ● ❖ ✖
✳ ⤴ ✦ ▲

Name:

Defining the Future

1   Looking Up the 'Future'

What does the word 'future' mean? First write your own definition and then check how the word 'future' is defined in at least two dictionaries. Add to your definition if needed.

Future _____

_____

_____

2   Finding 'Future' Words

Conduct a dictionary and thesaurus search for words that relate to the future, eg tomorrow, upcoming, later. Did you find at least 10 words you can list below?

1 _____   2 _____

3 _____   4 _____

5 _____   6 _____

7 _____   8 _____

9 _____   10 _____

3   Rewriting the Past

Select a favourite novel or short story and rewrite the opening paragraph (or a favourite part of the story) to move the action or event into the future. Use some of the words you found in your dictionary and thesaurus search.

_____

_____

_____

_____

_____

Name:

Alphabets for the Future

1   Alphabets or Gammabets?

Throughout the history of human civilization, people have devised ways of communicating in the written form. From your study of Ancient Civilizations, you have learned about some of the alphabets (or writing systems) that are still used today. Using the standard alphabet as a base, devise a new type of alphabet code or code for the future comprising shapes or symbols.

A _____   B _____   C _____   D _____   E _____   F _____   G _____

H _____   I _____   J _____   K _____   L _____   M _____   N _____

O _____   P _____   Q _____   R _____   S _____   T _____   U _____

V _____   W _____   X _____   Y _____   Z _____

2   Code Making and Breaking

Now that you have devised your new 'alphabet code' write a 'future' message to a friend. Give them time to work out your message before you let them see the code breaker. Teach your friends how to use your code.

_____

_____

_____

_____

3   Future Headlines

Use your 'future code' to write out a news report headline. Check if any of your classmates can decipher your headline.

Thinking Strategies for the Successful Classroom, 9–11 Year Olds   Brilliant Publications

Name:

Looking to the Future

GARDNER'S
MULTIPLE
INTELLIGENCES
Worksheet 55

1 Picturing the Future

How we picture the future is often influenced by films, television series, documentaries and books. List 10 films or books that are set in the future.

1 _____   2 _____

3 _____   4 _____

5 _____   6 _____

7 _____   8 _____

9 _____   10 _____

2 Now and Then

Consider all the things that might change in the future, eg transport, clothes, food, medicine, education etc. Record your ideas on the chart below:

How Things Are Today	How Things Could Be in the Future

Activities for the Future – Food

Future Food

In groups of three or four, discuss what food might be available in the future. Use pictures of food from magazines and supermarket catalogues to stimulate discussion.

Brainstorm ideas of what changes will take place in the food we eat. Record your ideas on a concept map.

Create a supermarket catalogue for shoppers in the future. What food will no longer be sold and why? Will there be new foods that are not available today? Will more information be included on ingredients and nutrition?

Future 'Fast Food'

It is 2055 and you have a great idea for a new fast-food outlet.

Create a name for your enterprise and design a logo that will be easy for people to see and remember.

What type of food will it sell? Design a poster promoting the exciting, new and 'so healthy' products you will sell.

Cooking up a Storm

Will food still need to be cooked in the future?

Invent a new piece of equipment that 'cooks' food ready for eating and retains all the essential vitamins and minerals.

Prepare a prototype, a model or a detailed plan of your invention.

Show your invention to an 'expert' and ask for feedback. Revise your plan based on the feedback you receive.

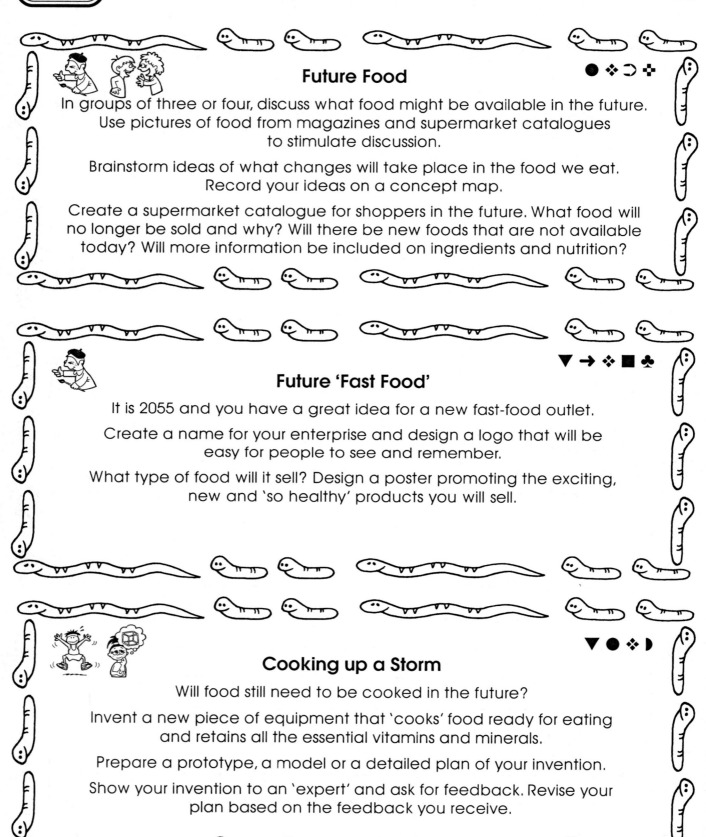

Activities for the Future – Entertainment

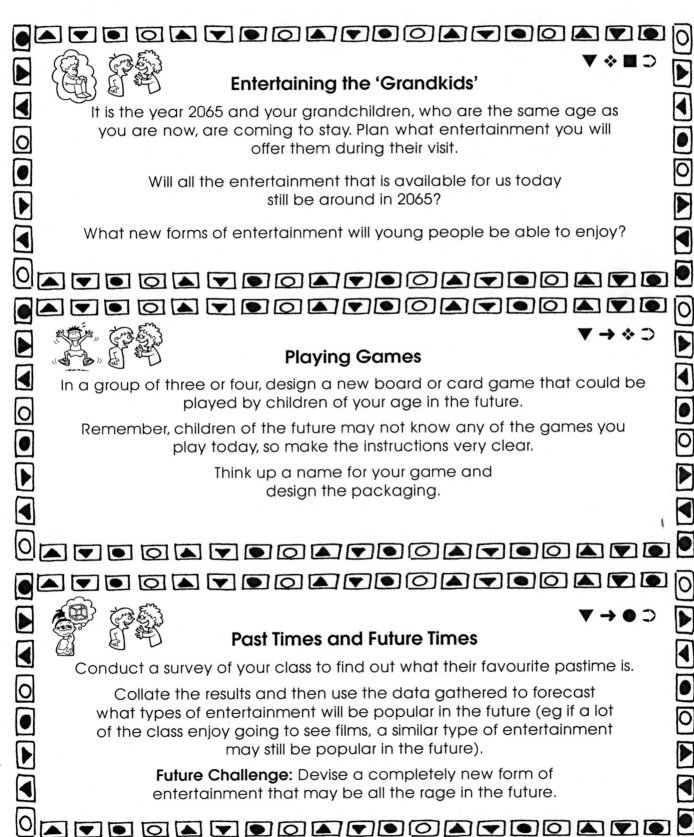

Entertaining the 'Grandkids'

It is the year 2065 and your grandchildren, who are the same age as you are now, are coming to stay. Plan what entertainment you will offer them during their visit.

Will all the entertainment that is available for us today still be around in 2065?

What new forms of entertainment will young people be able to enjoy?

Playing Games

In a group of three or four, design a new board or card game that could be played by children of your age in the future.

Remember, children of the future may not know any of the games you play today, so make the instructions very clear.

Think up a name for your game and design the packaging.

Past Times and Future Times

Conduct a survey of your class to find out what their favourite pastime is.

Collate the results and then use the data gathered to forecast what types of entertainment will be popular in the future (eg if a lot of the class enjoy going to see films, a similar type of entertainment may still be popular in the future).

Future Challenge: Devise a completely new form of entertainment that may be all the rage in the future.

Activities for the Future – Sport

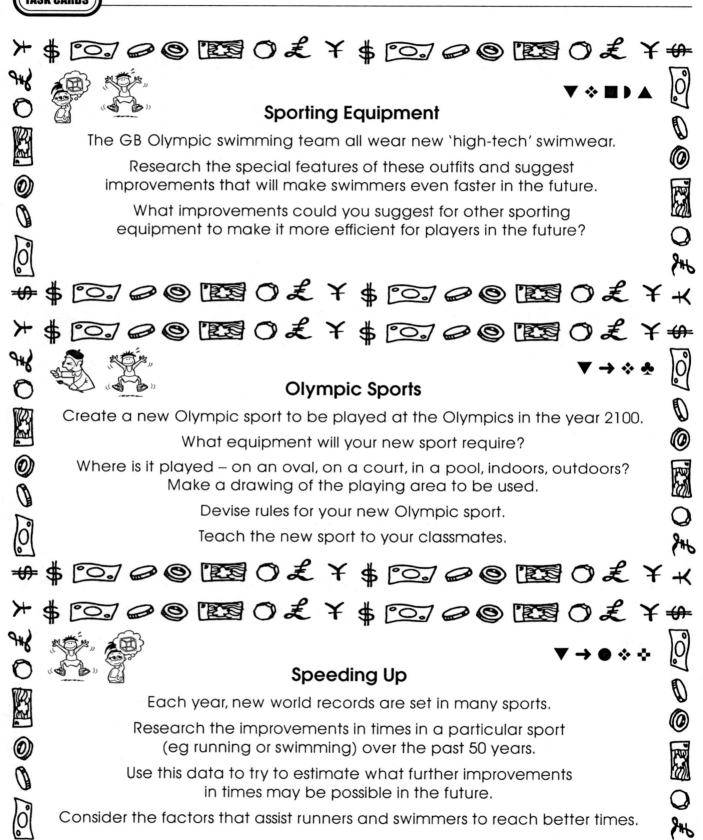

Sporting Equipment

The GB Olympic swimming team all wear new 'high-tech' swimwear.

Research the special features of these outfits and suggest improvements that will make swimmers even faster in the future.

What improvements could you suggest for other sporting equipment to make it more efficient for players in the future?

Olympic Sports

Create a new Olympic sport to be played at the Olympics in the year 2100.

What equipment will your new sport require?

Where is it played – on an oval, on a court, in a pool, indoors, outdoors? Make a drawing of the playing area to be used.

Devise rules for your new Olympic sport.

Teach the new sport to your classmates.

Speeding Up

Each year, new world records are set in many sports.

Research the improvements in times in a particular sport (eg running or swimming) over the past 50 years.

Use this data to try to estimate what further improvements in times may be possible in the future.

Consider the factors that assist runners and swimmers to reach better times.

This page may be photocopied for use by the purchasing institution only.
© Blake Education Pty Ltd. 2004

Activities for the Future – Transport

Public Transport

Make a list of all the types of transport available now.

What sort of public transport will there be in the future?

Plan a trip to another country in the year 2200. In order to reach your destination, you will have to change your transport method at least three times. What types of transport will you travel on?

Future of Fossil Fuels

Fossil fuels may not last far into the future. What alternative fuel or power source might be used by the end of the 21st century?

Design a vehicle that is powered by an alternative to fossil fuel.

Prepare and present a report that will persuade the government to invest in further development of your project.

Space Travel

In the future, people from Earth may visit or even live on one of the many planets in our solar system.

How will people travel the long distances into space in the future and what facilities will have to be built to cater for the type of transport used?

Although the distance into space may be greater than we are used to travelling on Earth, it may not take as long to get there. Draw up a timetable for a regular service to one or more of the planets in our solar system.

Activities for the Future – Government

Government of the Future ▼ ❖ ✶ ⊃ ✦ ▲

At present, the UK has a democratically elected government. What other countries in the world are democracies? Make an Alphabet Chart and list all these countries.

If you were still alive 200 years from now, what changes would you see in the way countries are governed?

Is it possible that there could be a 'worldwide government' that united all people?

Could Earth be part of an 'intergalactic alliance', joining with other planets to help govern our universe?

Conduct a class debate on the topic:

Government of the Future – United We Stand, Divided We Fall!

Votes ▼ ❖ ✖ ❱ ⊃

It is 2059 and you are a candidate in an upcoming election. What are the issues that are concerning voters?

Create a name and slogan for your political party.

What are your policies regarding health, education, the environment, business, trade and social welfare for 2059 and beyond?

Choose one of these major issues and develop three 'election promises' that you believe you can deliver.

Future Politicians ▼ → ❖ ✦ ▲

Some countries offer special education scholarships providing training and support to many promising young sportsmen and women.

What if those governments decided it was equally important to prepare our future politicians?

What qualities and talents would today's young people have to exhibit to be selected to attend the 'European Institute for Politicians of the Future'?

Brainstorm with a group of fellow 'potential politicians' what topics should be included in the curriculum.

Name: _____

Future Days

1   My Future Birthday

It is the year 2054. Describe how different your 11th birthday would be. Begin with when you wake up that morning.

6am	_____	12.30pm	_____
6.30am	_____	1pm	_____
7am	_____	1.30pm	_____
7.30am	_____	2pm	_____
8am	_____	2.30pm	_____
8.30am	_____	3pm	_____
9am	_____	3.30pm	_____
9.30am	_____	4pm	_____
10am	_____	4.30pm	_____
10.30am	_____	5pm	_____
11am	_____	5.30pm	_____
11.30am	_____	6pm	_____
12noon	_____	6.30pm	_____

2   A Letter to the Future YOU!

Write a letter to yourself to be opened on your 21st Birthday. Explain what you think your life will be like then. Include a drawing or photo of yourself now and maybe some items that will bring back memories for you at 21.

Dear _____

_____

_____

_____

Name:

Future Studies

1 Web Search

There are many individuals and organizations interested in studying and preparing for the future. Some of these groups share their ideas and opinions on the World Wide Web. Visit these three websites and write a brief review of each of the sites and their contents.

1 www.cotf.edu – The NASA Classroom of the Future

_____

_____

_____

2 www.facingthefuture.org

_____

_____

_____

3 www.spacefuture.com

_____

_____

_____

2 Planning for the Future

Name three organizations (other than the three above) that are concerned with planning for the future and explain why future planning is necessary for them.

	Organization	Reason for Future Planning
1.		
2.		
3.		

Printed in the United Kingdom
by Lightning Source UK Ltd.
127809UK00001B/167-238/A